OXFORD
INDIA SHORT
INTRODUCTIONS

CAPITAL FLOWS AND EXCHANGE RATE MANAGEMENT

The Oxford India Short
Introductions are concise,
stimulating, and accessible guides
to different aspects of India.
Combining authoritative analysis,
new ideas, and diverse perspectives,
they discuss subjects which are
topical yet enduring, as also
emerging areas of study and debate.

OTHER TITLES IN THE SERIES

The Indian Constitution
Madhav Khosla

Natural Disasters and Indian History
Tirthankar Roy

Caste
Surinder S. Jodhka

The Poverty Line
S. Subramanian

Water Resources of India
A. Vaidyanathan

Panchayati Raj
Kuldeep Mathur

The Right to Information in India
Sudhir Naib

Affirmative Action in India
Ashwini Deshpande

The Civil Services in India
S.K. Das

A part of the *Oxford India Short Introductions* series, this book belongs to a cluster of nine titles around the theme 'Economics and Development'. I have deliberately kept these two words separate. We tend to forget that the non-economic aspects of development have an important bearing on the economic aspects. The focus of the theme is how a country like India faces and solves (or fails to solve) various questions related to its quest for sustainable development. Moreover, every book within this cluster presents the reader with a quick recapitulation of the relevant theory so that opinions can be disentangled from conclusions based on theory.

Anindya Sen, Professor of Economics, Indian Institute of Management Kolkata; General Editor for the cluster on 'Economics and Development', *OISI*

Other Titles in the Cluster

Indian Cities
Annapurna Shaw

Monetary Policy
Partha Ray

Trade and Environment
Rajat Acharyya

OXFORD
INDIA SHORT
INTRODUCTIONS

CAPITAL FLOWS AND EXCHANGE RATE MANAGEMENT

SOUMYEN SIKDAR

OXFORD
UNIVERSITY PRESS

OXFORD
UNIVERSITY PRESS

Oxford University Press is a department of the University of Oxford.
It furthers the University's objective of excellence in research, scholarship,
and education by publishing worldwide. Oxford is a registered trademark of
Oxford University Press in the UK and in certain other countries

Published in India by
Oxford University Press
YMCA Library Building, 1 Jai Singh Road, New Delhi 110 001, India

ISBN-13: 978-0-19-807545-5
ISBN-10: 0-19-807545-6

Typeset in 11/15.6 Bembo Std
by Excellent Laser Typesetters, Pitampura, Delhi 110 034
Printed in India at G.H. Prints Pvt Ltd, New Delhi 110 020

Contents

Tables, Figures, and Boxes

Tables

Figures

Boxes

Introduction

Greater financial integration is a critical aspect of globalization. Ebbs and flows of foreign funds into the domestic stock market, acquisition of foreign companies by Indian business, memorandums of understanding (MoUs) signed by a state government with a multinational company that wants to set up or expand operations in the state, and similar issues get a great deal of attention in the news media. So do the rise and fall of the value of the rupee and changes in the dollar reserves of the Reserve Bank of India (RBI). The situation used to be drastically different even twenty years ago. The exchange rate of the rupee was kept artificially fixed in the open market by the RBI and there were a host of rules and regulations that prevented Indians from buying assets abroad and foreigners from investing in India, and nobody had a clear idea about the stock of dollars maintained by the RBI. Then came the great global wave of liberalization in the 1990s and many of these restrictions were swept away. Profitable investment opportunities opened up as governments in one country after another deregulated industries, privatized public sector units, and encouraged production for export. Foreign institutional investors (FIIs) such as mutual funds and pension funds were quick to grab this opportunity of earning higher returns and reducing risk through diversification. They had plenty of funds on hand and returns were very low in the advanced economies.

Our country is currently much more open to cross-border flows, of not only commodities and services, but also investible funds (also known as 'financial capital' or simply 'capital'). Like India, a large number of other developing economies also embraced economic reforms in the late 1980s and 1990s in a move to greater openness. In this group of nations, collectively known as the emerging market economies (EMEs), India has emerged as one of the most preferred destinations for foreign investors and is likely to remain so in the near future.

Alongside numerous benefits, greater global integration has inevitably brought several problems in its wake for developing countries. Unrestricted imports of goods have threatened domestic jobs and volatile flows of funds across national borders have created serious financial instability, often leading to devastating economic crises. The view dominating policy circles in powerful international institutions such as the World Bank and the International Monetary Fund (IMF) tends to extol the benefits while understating the costs of unrestricted cross-border flow of funds. Instead of encouraging careful supervision, nations are told that the only sensible course is to work towards the goal of completely unfettered international trade in financial assets. India has done well so far by not heeding this advice, but is under pressure to change its policy.

Access to the savings of foreigners can potentially be of great benefit to a developing country in which the low level of domestic savings acts as an impediment to investment. However, potential costs also have to be carefully weighed against the supposed benefits if a wise decision is to be made. There is enough evidence that, unless judiciously managed, cross-border movement of capital can act as a seriously disruptive force.

Even when there is no crisis, it tends to impose serious limits on the ability of national governments to use monetary, budgetary, and exchange rate related policies to achieve national goals. In a globalized world, managing the economy has become much more difficult.

The objective of this short introduction is to introduce the non-specialist reader to the fundamental economic issues related to this critical aspect of globalization. She will get an overall view of the basic forces driving capital flows, their impact on the exchange rate, and their implications for foreign reserves and domestic money supply. Indian policymakers have been successful in averting crisis and in maintaining high growth in an environment fraught with undesirable possibilities. This success stands in sharp contrast to the dismal performance of many Latin American and African countries. The book should be able to assist the reader in understanding and appreciating this success.

1

Types and Trends of Capital Flows

At any given point in time, Indian households and producers are continuously engaged in transactions with foreigners. These transactions may be broadly classified into two types: transactions of goods and services and transactions of financial assets. The former, for instance, can take the form of buying rice from Bangladesh, tea from Sri Lanka, or cars from Korea; selling garments to France; buying copper from Chile or oil from Saudi Arabia; watching Hollywood movies; travelling to Italy; or supplying restaurant meals and hotel accommodation to visiting Australian tourists. Examples of asset transactions would be, an Indian investor purchasing shares in a British company or depositing dollars in a New York bank, or an Indian company borrowing from a Japanese financial institution. In the first two instances, the Indian investor is acquiring some form of financial asset, company share certificates and certificate of deposit, respectively. In the third instance, the Japanese institution is acquiring an Indian asset, that is, a claim on future payments from the Indian company. The common feature of all these transactions is that the lenders (investors) give the borrowers funds to be used now in exchange for promises entitling them to interest and other returns later.

When an Indian citizen buys a computer from an American company that is also acquisition of an asset. At the same time, it is an import of a durable good. Throughout this text, the term 'asset trade' will be taken to mean transactions in financial assets only, and not trade in durable goods.

Transactions in financial assets are known as *capital flows*. 'Capital' here stands for financial funds (investible funds) and not machinery or equipment. When an Indian purchases a foreign asset, it is capital outflow or capital export from India (as funds flow out of the country to buy a foreign asset) and, conversely, when a foreigner purchases an Indian asset it is capital inflow or capital import into India. At this stage, there is no transfer of physical capital corresponding to the financial flows. Capital outflow from India to Thailand, for example, simply means that Indian investors have acquired shares, bonds, bank deposits, or other income-earning assets in Thailand. Likewise, capital inflow into India say, from Germany means that German investors have acquired income-yielding assets in this country. 'Capital flows', 'flow of funds and financial claims', and 'asset transactions' will be used interchangeably throughout the book.

Why is Asset Trade Beneficial?

Trade in financial assets is backed by the transfer of funds from lenders to borrowers. The borrower has a profitable investment opportunity but lacks the funds to execute it. Therefore, if she can borrow from the lender at terms acceptable to the latter, both gain. It is essentially similar to mutually beneficial exchanges between the buyers and the sellers of any commodity, for example, shirts. Instead of shirts, money and claims to future returns are changing hands. The lenders (investors) supply funds to be used for the present in exchange for entitlement to interest and dividends

3

later. In the financial market this entitlement or claim is traded: lenders buy it from borrowers. This type of trade contributes to social welfare by matching the supply of investible or loanable funds with its demand. Developing countries often have investment opportunities, but lack the funds to exploit them as low income implies low savings (supply of investible funds). With access to global financial trading, funds can be borrowed from abroad (utilizing foreign savings) to finance local investment. In the absence of asset trade, a country's investment is necessarily limited by its own local savings. The global capital market channels the world's savings to its most productive use, regardless of location, by taking advantage of varying rates of return in different countries.

Apart from procuring higher returns for the lender access to international opportunities creates a second source of gain: holding foreign assets lowers the riskiness of portfolio through greater *diversification*. When a country can participate in the international capital market, the riskiness of its wealth can be reduced by placing some of its 'eggs' in the additional foreign 'baskets'. A related gain stems from *consumption smoothing*. Normally, individuals prefer to have a smooth profile of consumption over time. Fluctuations in consumption tend to make them unhappy. Without any facility of borrowing or lending, a person's consumption will be determined by her current income and hence may widely fluctuate over time when income is prone to be variable. If borrowing and lending are possible, savings in good times (high income period) may be lent and the returns used in periods of low income to achieve a steady level of consumption in all periods. International asset transactions confer additional benefits by expanding the saver's set of available instruments. Thus, a country can reduce the risks of fluctuations in income and consumption by participating in international capital transactions.

In principle, the welfare effects of international borrowing and lending-asset transactions, in general, are exactly parallel to the effects of opening up of trade in goods and services. In either case the choice set available to a nation's citizens, either as consumers or as investors, gets enlarged and this enhances social welfare. Any government interference with either will constitute bad policy.

Unfortunately, the similarity between the exchange of shirts and of financial assets only holds up to a point.

5

The chief difference is that a large part of the international trade in assets is driven by expectations of quick, short-term gains. Such expectations can be rather fickle or volatile in nature, being in turn driven by fads and fashions, euphoria and panic. Goods once sold cannot be taken back, but financial flows are reversible. Historically, cross-border financial transactions have been characterized by recurrent episodes of mania and panic. Since finance is central to all economic activity, any turbulence in the financial field tends to spread quickly to other sectors. If the initial disturbance is large enough, the economy may soon find itself engulfed in a crisis. To make matters worse, such financial crisis in one country often spills over to the neighbouring region, producing contagion. Trade in commodities is usually not susceptible to such volatility and is much less crisis-prone than capital movements. Therefore, it may be wrong to treat goods trade and asset trade symmetrically and apply the same set of policies to them. Abolition of protectionism to encourage free trade in goods and services may be beneficial, but at the same time it may be prudent to retain control over capital movements to minimize the possibility of devastating crises. To give just one such instance, excessive

6

borrowing of foreign short-term capital lay at the heart of the Asian crisis of the late 1990s, as Indonesia, South Korea, and Thailand loosened up restrictions on international financial transactions and allowed their banks and companies to borrow recklessly from abroad. These economies have been helped by unfettered trade in the goods they export, but were terribly hurt by a simple extension of that policy to trade in financial assets.

Keeping this important lesson in mind, the following sections explore other aspects of capital flows.

Classification

Cross-border capital flows are conventionally classified into various categories by maturity (short-term/long-term), type of investor and borrower (private/official), and degree of managerial control (direct/portfolio). Conventionally, flows that mature after one year are treated as long-term. Internationally traded assets are of the following major forms.

Debt claims contractually stipulate fixed payments that borrowers have to make to their creditors. They can either be bonds that are marketable securities or

7

loans that are not usually marketable. Debts do not confer ownership rights.

By contrast, *equity* (or *stock*) entails ownership. Equity holders get a share of the enterprise's profits after the servicing of debt. If profit fluctuates, so will the equity holder's return, but the debt holder's return is contractually fixed and not subject to risk.

When equity or stock purchase implies 'direct control' over the management of the company selling the stock, it is called *foreign direct investment* (FDI). Since control is hard to quantify, conventionally, equity purchases amounting to at least 10 per cent of the value of the firm are treated as FDI. Buying and selling of equity not entailing control and of bonds constitute *foreign portfolio investment* (FPI). Among the different types of asset transactions, it is FDI that is directly linked to the addition of physical capital in the host country, and in this respect is fundamentally different from other types of flows. The distinguishing trait of FDI which is direct ownership and control, often involves setting up or expanding a subsidiary firm or factory in a foreign land (*greenfield investment*). It may also take the form of buying local enterprises or extending the foreign company's stake in these enterprises (*mergers and acquisitions*). An investment by IBM in its branch in Bangalore would be an example of a direct investment by the US in India. FDI is also distinct from other investments in that it often plays a major role in the transfer of technical knowledge and ideas across national boundaries.

Official flows consist of both long-term and short-term lending by a government or a multilateral institution like the World Bank or the IMF.

The distinction between debt and equity finance from foreign sources becomes very important in matters of repayment. In the event of an unforeseen development such as a recession, scheduled payments on debt obligations to foreigners do not fall, causing hardship to the country. If the blow is severe enough, there may actually be default. In the case of equity, on the other hand, decline in domestic income automatically reduces the earnings of foreign shareholders without violating any payment agreement. Equity holders effectively agree to share in both the good and the bad fortunes of the country. If foreign lenders fear default, new loans will not be forthcoming and old short-term loans may be recalled. This may make matters really serious for a country which is already reeling under a recession. Thus, greater reliance on debt rather than equity finance makes an economy more vulnerable to the risk of a lending crisis.

Measurement of FDI in India has undergone some important changes. The following box explains.

Box 1   Measuring India's FDI

FDI in India used to be defined in a way that did not conform to the international reporting norms set by the IMF as it was confined only to foreign equity capital reported on the basis of issue or transfer of equity or preference shares to foreign investors. Some important items that were excluded include-

1. Reinvested earnings by foreign companies which are part of foreign investment profits that are not distributed to shareholders as dividends and are retained and reinvested in the affiliates in the home country.

2. Investment made by international bodies in Indian companies as venture capital funds.

3. Grants given by the parent companies to their subsidiaries in India.

4. Control premium (premium paid to gain control of a company) paid by foreigners.

To conform to IMF standards (which China follows) RBI revised the data on FDI from 2000–2001 onwards to include 'reinvested earnings' and 'other capital' as two additional categories. While the former refers to retained earnings of foreign companies, the latter covers inter-corporate debt transactions between related entities.

As a result of this revision the yawning gap between FDI inflows into China and India has narrowed significantly. It should, however, be noted that even India's new definition leaves out several items included in IMF's list. The feasibility of including these items is being explored.

The Structure of the International Capital Market

The main agents of international asset transactions are commercial banks, business enterprises, institutional investors, central banks, and other government agencies.

Liabilities of commercial banks consist mainly of deposits of various maturities, while their assets consist mostly of loans to individuals, corporations and governments, and deposits at other banks (including the central bank). Investment banks underwrite issues of corporate stocks and bonds by agreeing, for a fee, to find buyers for those securities at a guaranteed price.

Corporations all over the world are regularly turning to foreign sources of funds to meet their investment needs. For this purpose, they may sell stocks (or shares) which give buyers an equity claim on the corporation's profits, or they may opt for debt finance by selling bonds to international banks and other institutional lenders. Bonds are frequently denominated in the currency of the financial centre (for example, New York, Frankfurt, or Tokyo) in which the bonds are traded.

FIIs such as mutual funds, pension funds, and insurance companies have become very important players in the international flow of funds as they have moved into foreign assets on a big scale to boost returns and for diversification.

Central banks of the world routinely buy and sell foreign exchange as part of their exchange rate policy. These interventions exert considerable influence in the global capital market. In addition, governments of developing countries and public sector units have often borrowed from foreign sources. Poland, Mexico,

Hungary, and Greece are examples of countries which have, at some point or other, been heavily indebted to foreign banks and institutional lenders.

Trends

In the field of international lending, Britain was the leader before World War I and the main borrowers were the newly settled countries like the US, Canada, Australia, and Argentina. Flows ceased during the turmoil of the war and afterwards the US emerged as the dominant creditor. During the 1920s, a large number of countries issued foreign bonds on a large scale in New York. Defaults were not unknown, but they were not very significant in terms of the sums involved. Massive defaults, particularly by the developing countries, became a serious problem during the Great Depression era of the 1930s. Not unexpectedly, cross-border fund flows took a nosedive and remained at a low level well into the 1960s. Inter-governmental loans constituted the major part of the flow to the developing world. National governments continued to heavily restrict and regulate private transactions of all types. The developed countries began to remove these

13

restrictions by the 1960s, but the developing world did not follow.

Private lending to the poorer countries picked up significantly in the 1970s, in the wake of the oil price shocks. Organization of the Petroleum Exporting Countries (OPEC) managed to raise the price of oil to almost three times its previous level. There was a big jump in the incomes of the oil-exporting countries and most of the additional saving was put into bonds or bank deposits in the US and other financial centres in the advanced countries. Flush with funds, private banks started looking for ways to recycle the 'petro dollars'. The capital-rich developed world did not offer prospects for further investment that were attractive enough in terms of return. In the developing world there was strong resistance to FDI by multinational enterprises (MNEs). Therefore, the MNEs were not keen on borrowing funds for additional investment abroad. Hence the banks were forced to lend outright to governments and business enterprises in the developing countries. Capital exports to nonoil producing developing nations registered a sharp jump. In the rush for higher returns, every bank tried to get there first and caution was thrown to the winds. Much of the lending went to projects that were poorly planned and incompetently executed. In 1982, Mexico declared that it would be unable to service its foreign debt. Brazil and other Latin American countries followed suit. The subsequent decade witnessed a repetition of such disturbances in Mexico (1994–5), Venezuela (1995), Hungary (1995), Indonesia, Malaysia, South Korea, and Thailand (1997–9), Czech Republic (1997), Brazil (1998–9), Russia (1998–2000), Turkey (2001), and Argentina (2001–2). These disasters drove home the painful realization that free movement of investible funds across national boundaries may not be an unmixed blessing. They offer considerable advantages, no doubt, but may also pose genuine hazards.

Starting from the early 1990s, capital flows (debt and equity) to the developing countries picked up again. One major driving force was the low interest rates in the US. Also, by this time the developing world as a whole has come to accept economic reforms as an essential pre-requisite for growth and considerably softened its traditional resistance to funds flowing in from foreign shores. Governments were deregulating industries, reducing import duties and quotas, and privatizing loss-making public sector enterprises. In the developed world individual investors were supplanted by rapidly growing groups of institutional investors (mainly mutual funds and pension funds). With huge funds at their disposal, they were constantly on the lookout for investment opportunities abroad to raise returns and reduce risk through diversification. They developed an insatiable appetite for the shares of stock of firms in countries committed to globalization. On the supply side, privatization of state enterprises in a growing number of countries has greatly expanded the menu of financial instruments available in national equity and bond markets for purchase by foreign portfolio investors.

There is one noteworthy difference compared with the lending surge of the 1970s. Bank lending was overtaken in importance by portfolio investment in stocks and bonds. The major destinations for investment were the emerging economies of Asia and Latin America—China, Indonesia, Malaysia, South Korea, Thailand, Argentina, Brazil, and Mexico. In recent years, India has become a major destination for portfolio investment.

India's Experience

After independence, India wanted to build a strong industrial base as quickly as possible. It was felt, not entirely without justification, that indigenous manufacturing would not be able to grow without protection against foreign competition. A similar strategy was followed by all the developed countries in the early phases of their development. As a result of this policy, India's regulation of cross-border transactions, of goods and services as well as financial assets, became both extensive and stringent. High import duties and quantitative controls on import of consumer goods became the norm and investments by foreigners were almost totally banned barring deposits by non-resident Indians. High import duties supplemented by licensing and quotas placed Indian industries among the most protected in the world. An inevitable consequence was inefficiency and inability and unwillingness to compete in world markets. The exchange rate of the rupee was kept under strict control and not allowed to respond to the market forces of demand and supply. This inward-looking policy provided desired insulation against external disturbances for a long time.

17

With the growth of industrial production under state patronage and the adoption of fertilizer-intensive technology in agriculture, import of petroleum products, industrial components and, raw materials increased at a rapid pace. Exports were languishing due to the lack of competitive strength. A large deficit in the balance of payments was inevitable. External debt and debt servicing obligations mounted. The massive shock of the Gulf War culminated in the crisis of 1989–91. The Government of India (GoI) was forced to seek financial help from the IMF and other sources. Under pressure from these organizations, an ambitious and comprehensive programme of reforms was initiated across all sectors. The earlier protectionist policy stance was largely abandoned.

To reverse the growing inefficiency, the economy was opened up to foreign competition and the plethora of controls on trade in goods and services were quickly lifted. A cautious step-by-step approach was adopted for liberalization of capital flows (removal of restrictions on trade in financial assets); but even here relaxations were substantial. Select Indian companies were permitted to raise funds from the international capital market and measures were taken to encourage

> **BOX 2**   Convertible Currency
>
> A convertible currency is one that may be freely exchanged for foreign currencies. Convertibility can be of two types. The rupee is fully convertible on the current account, meaning that now there are virtually no restrictions on the purchase and sale of foreign exchange by private parties for trade in goods and services. However, trade in assets is still very carefully regulated. There are restrictions on the types of international capital transactions that private residents can undertake. In other words, *capital controls* still exist. This means that the rupee is not convertible on the capital account yet. Since integration with the global capital market is a central pillar of globalization, GoI has adopted a policy of gradually moving towards full capital convertibility in the near future.

foreign investment (both FPI and FDI). Exchange control was lifted and the rupee was made convertible on the current account in 1994.

Table 1 shows the net capital inflows (inflow minus outflow) as a percentage of the gross domestic product (GDP) for India over a number of years.

TABLE 1 Net Capital Inflow Ratios for India

	Net FDI/GDP	Net FPI/GDP	Total Net Inflow/GDP
2000–1	0.69	0.55	1.24
2001–2	0.96	0.40	1.36
2002–3	0.62	0.18	0.80
2003–4	0.39	1.84	2.23
2004–5	0.52	1.29	1.81
2005–6	0.36	1.50	1.86
2006–7	0.81	0.74	1.55
2007–8	1.28	2.21	3.49
2008–9	1.63	−1.15	0.48
2009–10	1.36	2.35	3.71
2010–11	0.41	1.72	2.13

Source: Reserve Bank of India.

The figures show a sustained increase of FDI and FPI flows since 2005–6. Also, since 2003–4, (with the exception of 2008–9, the severest year of the global crisis, when net portfolio flows actually turned negative) portfolio investment has come to dominate direct investment. The drop in net FDI in recent years is largely due to sustained increase in outward FDI flows from the country.

2

Balance of Payments, Exchange Rate, and Monetary Policy

Balance of Payments: A Brief Introduction

The balance of payments (BoP) is a systematic record of all transactions between the economic units of one country (households, firms, and the government) and the rest of the world. It consists of three major parts: the current account, the capital account, and changes in official international reserves.

The major items in the current account include export and import of goods and services and income flows during the current period. Trade in services has become very important in recent years. When an American company pays for an Indian consultant or advertising agent in Bangalore or a tourist from

Thailand spends on hotel rooms, meals, and transportation in Agra, India receives payments for exporting services. In addition, India trades in insurance, shipping, education, financial, and technical services of different kinds. Transactions in services are often called 'invisible', because their movement is not visible across national borders.

Income flows are payments to holders of assets. India earns returns on foreign assets held by Indians and makes payment to foreigners who hold Indian assets. Unilateral transfers also figure in the current account. One kind of private transfer, which is relatively important for India, is the remittance made by Indian migrants working abroad. The current account is in surplus if the value of exports, plus inward income flow, plus transfers exceeds the value of imports, plus outward income flows, plus transfers.

The capital account records transactions in financial assets. The values reported here are only for the principal amounts of the assets bought and sold. The flows of earnings on assets such as interest income are reported under income flows in the current account.

The basic BoP accounting rule is: any transaction leading to a receipt of foreign exchange creates a surplus (credit) and any transaction leading to payment to foreigners creates a deficit (debit) in the corresponding account. When India sells a shirt to Germany it earns foreign exchange and so counts as a credit in the current account. Import of petroleum is a debit as it involves payment of foreign currency. A foreign resident purchasing an Indian asset (a stock or a bond of an Indian company or a certificate of deposit in an Indian bank) is a credit in India's capital account as the Indian seller (borrower) is receiving payment from a foreigner. Funds are flowing into India, a capital export. An Indian purchasing a foreign asset is a debit in India's capital account because she is buying (importing) something from a foreigner and funds are flowing out of her home country. Surplus in the capital account means funds are flowing into the country, but unlike a surplus in the current account, the incoming flows are borrowings or sales of assets rather than earnings. Deficit in the capital account implies that funds are flowing out of the country, but also that the nation is increasing its claim on foreign assets.

Table 2 gives a summary statement of India's balance of payments for the year 2009–10. The current account balance and the capital account balance (both in US$ million) was −38,383 and 53,397 respectively. The sum of current balance, plus capital balance, plus errors and omissions is the overall balance (13,441). This will equal the change in official reserves. Positive

TABLE 2 India's BoP (US$ million)

Current Account	
Exports	1,82,235
Imports	3,00,609
Trade balance	−1,18,374
Invisibles	79,991
Non–factor services	35,726
Income	−8,040
Transfers	52,305
Current account balance	−38,383
Capital Account	
Capital account balance	53,397
External assistance (net)	2,893
External commercial borrowings (net)	2,808
Short–term debt	7,558
Banking capital (net) of which:	2,084
Non–resident deposits (net)	2,924
Foreign investments (net) of which:	51,167
FDI (net)	18,771
Portfolio (net)	32,396
Other flows (net)	−13,113
Errors and omissions	−1,573
Overall balance	13,441
Reserves increase (−)/decrease (+)	(−)13,441

Source: Economic Survey 2010–11.

capital balance signifies that the claim on our assets by foreigners went up in that particular year and that our country was a net borrower from abroad.

Conventionally, in the capital account, an increase in a country's foreign assets is a debit entry and carries a minus sign, while a decrease in foreign assets is a credit entry and carries a plus sign. Therefore the increase in reserves in the last line of the table carries a minus sign. Positive overall balance of 13,441 implies that, in that particular year, India's foreign reserves increased by that amount.

Official international reserves are foreign currencies or assets that are accepted by all governments in the settlement of international transactions. In the nineteenth and early twentieth centuries, gold was the universal official reserve asset following which its position was taken over by pound sterling. Since World War I, the US dollar has become the reserve asset for a majority of countries.

The BoP of a country will be in balance or in *equilibrium* (neither deficit nor surplus) if the receipts from all accounts match the expenditures. For convenience of exposition, we assume that all cross-border transactions are carried out in US dollars. Another way of stating this is, for the BoP to be in equilibrium, the demand for dollars should equal its supply. Indians wanting to import goods will sell rupees to buy dollars to pay the suppliers abroad while tourists visiting India sell dollars to buy rupees that can be spent in India. Similarly, if a foreign multinational company intends to buy stocks or bonds issued by an Indian entity or expand its operations in Gujarat, it will convert dollars into rupees. An Indian bank wishing to make a dollar deposit in New York will sell rupees to buy dollars. Thus *demand for dollar* or foreign exchange arises as a result of import of goods and services and outflow of capital–expansion of overseas operations of domestic corporations (FDI) or purchase of stocks, bonds, and securities by domestic investors (FPI). Export of goods and services from India creates a demand for rupees and supply of dollars, as foreign importers exchange dollars into rupees to pay for their imports. Similarly, FDI or FPI in Indian assets by foreigners generates dollar supply and rupee demand. Thus *supply of dollar* or foreign exchange arises as a result of export of goods and services and inflow of capital into the domestic country. Using the symbols X, M, CI, and CO to denote the values of export, import, capital inflow, and capital outflow, the condition of BoP in equilibrium may be written as:

$$X + CI = M + CO \qquad (1)$$

The left hand side of the equation gives the value of dollar supply in the rupee–dollar market while the right hand side provides the corresponding demand. A fruitful way of looking at equation (1) is to regard the left hand side as the source of foreign exchange and the right hand side as its use. Since rupee is obtained only in exchange for dollar and vice versa, dollar supply and rupee demand or rupee supply and dollar demand are two sides of the same coin. Expressed differently, if payments balance is attained in dollar, it is automatically attained in rupee as well. It should be noted that in equation (1) we are considering *private* flows only. If there are official transactions (usually by a central bank), the relation will have to be modified, as shown in the section 'Balance of Payments, Central Bank Intervention, and Money Supply'.

One important fact to be noted is that in the post-liberalization global currency market, international financial flows (capital account transactions CI and CO) are far more important than flows generated by exports and imports of goods and services (current account transactions X and M). It has been estimated that currently, foreign exchange trading by US dealers with non-financial customers is not more than 20 per cent of the total volume traded.

Current account deficit equals the excess of imports over the sum of exports and net transfers received from a country. This deficit must be covered by borrowing from foreigners or by selling assets to them. If India's current account deficit in a particular period is $10 million, it must be financed by net capital inflow, that is, excess of capital inflow over outflow amounting to $10 million. With *CAD* denoting current account deficit and *NCI* denoting net capital inflow, equation (1) may be restated as

$$CAD = NCI$$

In case this balance is disturbed by changes in *NCI*, the net flow of funds into India, *CAD*, will have to adjust accordingly. For example, if there is a fall in *NCI*, current account deficit will have to be brought down either through a rise in exports X or a fall in imports M or both. The first may take time, and the second may be costly in terms of loss of output, if essential imports such as petroleum or raw materials have to be curtailed. This has contemporary relevance because outward FDI by Indian companies has been rising steadily in recent years. Examples include Tata Steel buying Corus, Tata Motors acquiring Jaguar Land Rover, Hindalco buying Novelis, and ONGC acquiring Imperial Energy. These outbound cross-border deals are exerting a considerable downward push on NCI. Attempting to neutralize this, GoI is relaxing capital inflow norms to attract foreign funds. Otherwise, financing our current account deficit at an unchanged exchange rate will be a problem. In November 2011, the Finance Ministry raised the limits on foreign investment in government securities to $15 billion, and in corporate bonds to $20 billion.

Definition of Exchange Rate

The rupee–dollar exchange rate refers to the amount of rupees that can be exchanged for one dollar. For example, a rupee–dollar exchange rate of 40 implies that one dollar can be exchanged for 40 rupees, a rupee–euro exchange rate of 35 implies that one euro will exchange for 35 rupees, and similarly for other currencies. A rise in the exchange rate is a *depreciation* of the home currency—more units of the home currency are needed to purchase one unit of the foreign currency (a weaker rupee). The opposite of depreciation is *appreciation* (fall in the exchange rate, a stronger rupee).

When we say that the price of a shirt is Rs 250, what we mean is that Rs 250 will exchange for one shirt. Thus the rupee–dollar exchange rate is nothing but the price of dollar and the rupee–euro exchange rate is the price of euro, in terms of rupee. A rise in the rupee–dollar exchange rate is an increase in the price of dollar, which is equivalent to a decrease in the price of rupee or depreciation of rupee relative to dollar. Similarly, a decrease in the rupee–euro exchange rate is a fall in the price of euro or an increase or appreciation in the price of rupee relative to euro. In common parlance, 'price' and 'value' mean the same thing.

The rupee–dollar exchange rate is a bilateral rate between two currencies. In the presence of several currencies (say A, B, C, and D) the *effective exchange rate* of the rupee is defined as the weighted average of the exchange rates of the rupee against A, B, C, and

D. The weights used are the shares of countries with currencies A, B, C, and D in India's trade. The effective rate is multilateral rather than bilateral. Suppose that India trades only with the US (share 60 per cent) and the UK (share 40 per cent) and the bilateral exchange rates are 50 for the dollar and 10 for the pound. Then the effective exchange rate of the rupee equals 0.6 (50) + 0.4 (10) = 34. For Rs 34 one can buy a basket consisting of 0.6 dollars and 0.4 pounds.

In calculating the effective exchange rate (EER) unimportant trade partners are usually excluded. For example , only the top ten trade partners of India may be considered. The resulting EER is a 10-country (or 10-currency) EER for India. The shares used to weight the bilateral exchange rates may be the shares of the respective countries in the total export or total import or total trade (value of export plus import) of the home country.

EER is usually expressed as an index with 100 assigned as the value in a chosen base year and stated in such a way that an increase means an appreciation of the home currency with respect to the other currencies as a whole. For example, Economic Survey

2009 stated that the 6-currency EER declined from 112.16 in April 2008 to 95.65 in March 2009 due to significant depreciation of the rupee against the dollar, euro and yen. (The other three currencies are UK pound, Chinese renminbi and Hong Kong dollar).

Box 3   Spot and Forward Rates

What has been defined earlier is actually the spot exchange rate. This is the rate applicable to transactions involving immediate delivery or delivery within two days. The forward rate, in contrast, applies to agreements for an exchange of two currencies at an agreed date in future. The date as well as the rate of exchange between the currencies are fixed in advance at the time of writing the contract.

The chief utility of forward rates is that it provides protection against the risk of loss created by possible variations in the spot rate. The source of this risk is the delivery lag in international transactions. Consider an Indian company importing personal computers from the US. It will take thirty days for the consignment to arrive. The price of a PC is $100. If the rupee–dollar spot rate remains fixed, the buyer would know with certainty how much to pay in terms of rupees at the time of delivery. But fluctuations in the exchange rate over time create an exchange risk. Suppose the current rate is $E = 30$ (30 rupees per dollar) and the domestic price of a PC is Rs 40,000. Then profit per PC is Rs 37,000. If, however, the rupee depreciates to a spot rate of 40 on the date of delivery, the profit will fall to Rs 36,000. The importer can eliminate this risk by entering into a 30-day forward contract with a bank. If the 30-day forward rate is 35 rupees per dollar, he will be paid dollars for rupees at this rate at the time of payment, regardless of the spot rate on that date. By buying dollar (selling rupee) forward, the company will enjoy a guaranteed profit of Rs 36,500 per PC, minus the bank's fee for the service.

Determination of the Exchange Rate

We have seen that the exchange rate between two currencies may be understood as the price of one currency in terms of another. Being a price, its value will depend on and respond to pressures of demand and supply just as in the case of any other commodity. If the demand for a particular type of shirt or brand of wheat exceeds supply at the current price, there will be pressure on the price to go up, and if supply exceeds demand, the price will tend to fall. The same principle operates in the market for national currencies.

For the sake of simplicity, we assume that India trades only with the US, so that the rupee–dollar rate is the only exchange rate and the dollar is the only foreign currency for India. As already noted, demand for dollars arises as a result of our import of goods and services and purchase of foreign assets and supply of dollars is created by the export of goods and services and sale of assets to foreigners. When demand and supply are equal in foreign exchange transactions, value of imports plus capital outflows is equal to value of exports plus capital inflows. The BoP is in equilibrium. When demand for forex exceeds supply, it is in deficit and when supply exceeds demand, it is in surplus. Deficit or surplus signals that BoP is in disequilibrium, in which case, some variable will have to adjust. It is either the exchange rate under a flexible exchange system or the central bank's stock of foreign reserves (official reserves) under a fixed exchange system. The two systems are explained in the sections that follow.

Demand for commodities such as wheat or shirts typically responds inversely to change in price while supply responds directly to it. In other words, as price rises, demand falls and supply increases. Graphically, it means that when plotted against price, the demand schedule will have a negative slope and the supply schedule, a positive slope. The same should hold for demand and supply of dollars in response to changes in the price of dollar, which is nothing but the exchange rate.

To understand the logic behind the slope of the supply curve for dollars, imagine that the exchange rate has increased from 35 to 40. Before the increase, a shirt priced at Rs 350 in Delhi would cost an American tourist $10. After the rise in the exchange rate, the same shirt will cost only $350/40, less than $10. Sales, that is, our exports will go up. This can be generalized for all exports. To pay for more exports, Americans will need rupees, and will supply dollars to obtain those rupees. A rise in the price of dollar results in increased supply of it. Hence the supply curve slopes up. To see the effect on demand for dollars, consider an Indian purchasing in Delhi a burger imported from New York. The dollar price is $2. After the rise in the exchange rate, the price in rupee units goes up from Rs 70 to Rs 80, leading to less consumption (import) by Indians.

The demand for dollar required to pay for imports falls following the rise in its price. The demand curve slopes down. Since the same logic applies to assets also, we are justified in drawing the curves in Figure 1.

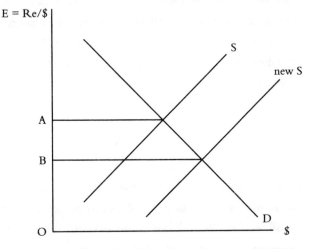

FIGURE 1 Value of the Exchange Rate under Flexible Exchange System: Effect of a Supply Increase

Flexible Exchange System

The simplest system is the flexible or floating exchange system in which the government or the central bank (RBI in our case) does not intervene. (The terms 'flexible exchange system', 'floating exchange system', and 'free float' are used interchangeably.) The exchange rate, or spot price of foreign exchange, is entirely market-driven; determined by the interaction of private demand and private supply of dollars. The value of the exchange rate in such a system is one that clears the market by equating demand and supply. In Figure 1 it is depicted as OA. Only at this value of the exchange rate, called the equilibrium value, demand equals supply and BoP is in equilibrium. If the rate is higher, supply will exceed demand (surplus in the BoP) and at a lower rate, demand will exceed supply (deficit in the BoP).

What makes the flexible exchange rate rise or fall over time? Such fluctuations are explained by forces that make the curves shift their positions. Let us look at the supply side. An increase in the US demand for made-in-India products or services will increase the demand for rupees, which is the same as an increase in the supply of dollars. In the figure, the supply curve shifts to the right, and at the new equilibrium, the value of the exchange rate is lower (OB rather than OA). If foreign investors want to buy more shares in Indian companies or expand production or marketing facilities in India, the outcome will be the same. Extra dollars will flow into the currency market to buy more rupees, and under free float (flexible exchange), the exchange rate or price of dollar will be pushed down. Fall in dollar price is an appreciation of the rupee.

Let us now consider a change from the demand side. If for some reason foreign goods or assets become more attractive to Indians, demand for dollars to make the necessary purchase will rise. This is shown as a rightward movement of the dollar demand curve in Figure 2. The exchange rate rises from OA to OC. This rise in the price of dollar is a depreciation of the rupee.

Let us use this analysis to examine the spectacular depreciation of the rupee during the second half of 2011. The rupee fell, or the price of dollar rose, from a value of 44.04 in August to an all-time low of 53.40 per dollar in December. Both demand and supply side factors contributed to this massive slide. Our exports were impacted adversely by the crisis in Europe, while the increase in oil price raised the cost of imports. At the same time, there was flight of capital from India. The slowdown of growth, depressed company profits, the decision to not allow

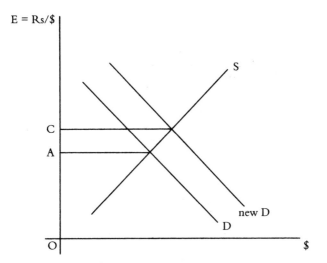

FIGURE 2 Effect of Increased Demand for
Foreign Exchange

FDI in retail and insurance, and fall in the Index of
Industrial Production (IIP)—all these factors combined to lower the optimism of foreign investors
about India. Indian assets, mainly equities, were sold
off on a large scale and the funds moved to safe-havens
like the US assets and gold. In terms of equation (1),
X and CI went down and M and CO went up simultaneously. This double blow—drop in supply of dollar
($X+CI$) plus rise in demand for it ($M+CO$)—caused

the sharp appreciation of the dollar and depreciation of the rupee.

Fixed Exchange System

In a flexible exchange system, the central bank does nothing to influence the exchange rate. On the other hand, in the fixed (or pegged) exchange system, the central bank of a country fixes the value of the exchange rate. It is price control imposed by the government in the market for foreign exchange. Since the fixed price will usually differ from the current market-clearing price, there must be official intervention to support the fixed price. The central bank must stand ready to buy or sell rupees and dollars at the announced target or pegged rate.

Completely fixed and completely flexible exchange rates are two extreme systems. Most countries, including India, follow a middle path of *managed exchange* or *managed float* where the central bank intervenes to keep fluctuations in the exchange rate under control. This is needed because too much fluctuation in such a crucial price as the exchange rate may damage the smooth functioning of an economy by making planning difficult. The RBI keeps a close watch on the movements of the price of rupee and monitors it without a fixed or pre-announced band within which variations will be tolerated. Over roughly the past decade, with the major exception of the period August–December of 2011, the management of the exchange rate has mostly taken the form of containing the upward pressure on the value of the rupee (downward pressure on the exchange rate).

Taking up the case of fixed exchange, consider Figure 3A which reproduces the demand–supply curves of Figure 1.

Suppose the exchange rate has been fixed at OF. Since this is higher than OA we say that the dollar is 'overvalued', or the rupee is 'undervalued', relative to its market-clearing level. At this value, the supply of dollar exceeds its demand (the gap TK). Unless this is removed from the market, the price of dollar will fall towards its equilibrium value under the pressure of excess supply. To prevent this and keep the exchange rate at the announced value OF, the central bank will have to buy, in exchange for rupee, dollars (of amount TK) from the market. This intervention fills the gap between non-official supply and demand and total

41

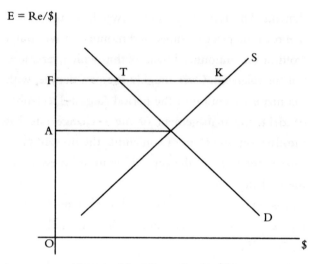

FIGURE 3A   Overvalued Dollar

demand (official plus non-official) will equal available supply at the announced value of the exchange rate. The central bank's stock of dollars will increase because of the purchase.

The other case of defense of a fixed exchange rate is also shown in Figure 3B. The official rate OF is below the equilibrium level OA. The dollar is 'undervalued' and the rupee 'overvalued' at this pegged rate. Dollar demand exceeds supply by MN. To defend this rate, officials must intervene in the foreign exchange market and sell dollars (of amount MN) from its stock of reserves to bring total supply (official as well as non-official) at an equal level with demand at this rate. But as the stock of foreign currency reserves gets depleted continuously, it may not be possible to keep the price indefinitely fixed at this level. Since RBI cannot print dollars, support will have to be withdrawn, once the stock gets exhausted or falls to an unacceptably low level. If support is given up, market forces will drive the exchange rate all the way up to OA.

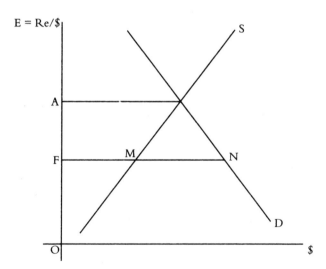

FIGURE 3B Undervalued Dollar

So far we have assumed that the exchange rate is rigidly fixed at OF. In reality, however, countries are happy if fluctuations in the exchange rate can be kept under control within some bounds. This is known as a 'target zone system'. Figure 4 provides an illustration.

The upper limit of the target zone is OG and the lower limit is OH, meaning that the central bank will intervene only if the exchange rate rises above OG or falls below OH. Consider a sudden rise in the demand for dollar that shifts the demand curve to the right.

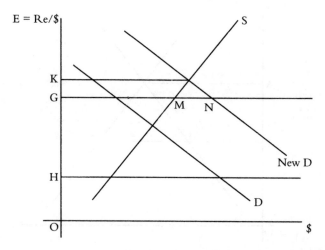

FIGURE 4   Target Zone System

Without intervention, the exchange rate will rise all the way to OK, but now it is not allowed to move beyond OG. At that level, demand for dollar exceeds supply by MN. Only this much has to be supplied by the central bank from its stock. Hence the depletion of reserves is lower compared to the situation of fixed targeting. In this way, the existence of some flexibility enhances the sustainability of a fixed rate system. But if the demand change is permanent, and nothing changes on the supply side, the reserve stock of dollars will continue to shrink and eventually reach an unacceptably low level.

India's Rising Reserves

In recent years, India's dollar reserves have reached very high levels. Their steady growth since 1991 was interrupted only by the dip in 2008, when capital flows dried up, following the global financial crisis. At that point, RBI had to sell dollars to prevent rupee depreciation. With the passing of the crisis, foreign funds started returning to India and, the policy of buying dollar was resumed. Reserve accumulation is the direct consequence of RBI's exchange rate policy.

TABLE 3   Forex Reserves of Some Major Countries (US$ billion) in December 2011

China	3,180
Japan	1,303
Saudi Arabia	541
Russia	514
Brazil	366
Germany	263
India	320

Source: Economic Survey 2010–11.

Attracted by the prospect of higher returns, foreign savers are buying Indian assets on a big scale, particularly shares of companies performing well. Under free float, this huge capital inflow would drive the exchange rate to a very low level, implying a sharp appreciation of the rupee. A strong upward push to the dollar price of Indian products will have a considerable adverse impact on the price competitiveness of the country's exports. Also, remittances from abroad will be strongly discouraged. Mainly to avoid this, the RBI steps in to prevent currency appreciation triggered by surges in the inflow of funds from abroad. This can be illustrated using the demand–supply graph once again in Figure 5.

Suppose that initially BoP is at equilibrium with the exchange rate at OA and the RBI wants to keep it

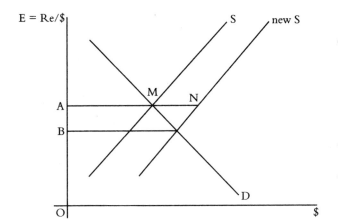

FIGURE 5 Dollar Purchase by a Central Bank

at that level. Additional foreign funds in the domestic stock market push the dollar supply curve to the right and the market-clearing value of the exchange rate sinks to OB. The rupee is stronger against the dollar. This is deemed undesirable because of its possible negative impact on exports and remittances. To prevent the exchange rate from falling, RBI buys up MN amount of dollars from the market. This will add to the stock of its foreign reserves. If the situation persists, the stock will keep on rising.

Accumulating a large stock of reserves is justified on precautionary grounds. It provides a cushion against potential disruptions to foreign trade and flow of funds which may cause serious damage to the economy. This precautionary motive has lately been strengthened by the perception of instability in a deregulated financial environment. (We return to this later.) A comfortable position in respect of foreign assets is also interpreted by foreign investors as a sign of sound health of the economy. Improvement in the credit rating of a nation enables it to access the international capital market on more favourable terms. Continuous addition to foreign currency reserves has facilitated further liberalization of restrictions on cross-border current and capital account transactions.

On the other hand, a continuously rising stock of reserves is bad, because it means that investible funds are not being used for productive purposes. Typically reserves are used to buy US Treasury bills, an asset that is very safe but yields a very low rate of return. Returns on profitable domestic projects in a capital poor country, on the other hand, tend to be much higher. This forgone return is one important cost of holding foreign reserves that must be balanced against its benefit as cushion against possible financial crisis and as an instrument for protecting domestic exporters against currency appreciation. Furthermore, large reserves tend to attract criticism from other countries that are running deficits with the reserve holding country. China's recent trade disputes with the US amply bear this out.

So what is the appropriate or optimal level of reserves that a country should maintain? There is no one solution that will fit all countries at all times. The traditional thumb rule was based on the notion of import cover: a country needs to maintain a minimum level of reserves, that is sufficient to pay for three months of imports. With the growing importance of capital account financial flows as the main source of instability and crisis, a new thumb rule has been proposed: a country should have enough reserves to cover all debt which would be due over the next year, in the event creditors suddenly become unwilling to roll it over or extend new loans. Sudden halts and reversals of foreign investment are more likely for foreign portfolio investment ('hot money'). Foreign direct investment is long-term in nature and guided by long-term profit considerations. Volatility is considerably lower as a result. When short-term flows dominate cross-border capital movements, the reserves need to be correspondingly large. Investment in India is dominated by short-term portfolio flows. (See Table 1). Therefore, the RBI cannot afford to have a low level of reserves.

It must, however, be recognized that even high reserves are no guarantee against turbulence in the currency market. Even the Bank of Japan and other central banks with substantial foreign reserves have failed to prevent large swings in the exchange rate and to preserve stability. The main reason for this failure lies in the sheer size of foreign exchange transactions relative to foreign reserves. The volume of foreign currency trading exceeds $2 trillion per day, which is bigger than the combined foreign exchange reserves of the rich countries. It is highly doubtful whether even China's mountain of dollars will be sufficient to ward off financial panic and crisis. Therefore, the case for controlling non-FDI capital flows becomes compellingly strong.

Balance of Payments, Central Bank Intervention, and Money Supply

In an economy, operating a fixed exchange rate, there is a close link between BoP and the domestic financial sector. In a flexible exchange system, the exchange rate is determined entirely by the forces of demand and supply of foreign exchange. Demand and supply will be equated and BoP will attain equilibrium through changes in the exchange rate. There is no need for outside intervention. However, in a fixed exchange system, the central bank will have to buy and sell dollars to support the fixed rate.

To support an overvalued rupee, the RBI will have to sell dollars from its stock in exchange for rupees. This will withdraw rupees from circulation and the domestic money supply will fall. For example, suppose that the RBI decides to sell $100 from its reserves to X in exchange for $100 of the home currency, which equals Rs 4000 assuming an exchange rate of 40. X pays in cash. The transaction has two effects. First, it reduces RBI's foreign reserves by $100. Second, currency in circulation falls by Rs 4000 (= $100). If instead of paying cash, X writes a cheque for Rs 4,000 on his State Bank of India (SBI) account, then the RBI reduces the reserves that SBI has to maintain at RBI by Rs 4000. Since SBI has to maintain a fixed ratio between its reserves at the RBI and its total deposits (the cash reserve ratio), it will have to contract the volume of its deposits by recalling loans. This will reduce the supply of money in the system. Thus, the purchase of dollar (sale of rupee) leads to an expansion of money supply and sale of dollar (purchase of rupee) leads to a contraction in money supply. Actually, RBI's sale and purchase of foreign exchange is no different in its impact on money supply from sale or purchase of any other asset, such as government bonds, held in its portfolio.

When a central bank intervenes in the foreign currency market the fundamental BoP relationship $X + CI = M + CO$ is altered. Any discrepancy between private dollar supply (left hand side) and private dollar demand (right hand side) will induce buying or selling of dollar by the central bank. Suppose that the supply is \$500 whereas demand is only \$300. Without intervention, the excess supply of dollars will tend to push down the value of the dollar, which is the same as rupee appreciation. To prevent this, the RBI will have to buy \$200 from the market. Its foreign reserves will go up by this amount. If in contrast supply was \$300 and demand \$500, under free float, the rupee will depreciate. RBI's prevention will involve selling \$200 from its stock to bridge the gap. Foreign reserves will go down by the same value. Change in reserves is positive in the case of purchase and negative in the case of sale. In the light of this and denoting reserve change by RC, we restate equation (1) as

$$X + CI = M + CO + RC \qquad (2)$$

In the first situation, $X + CI = \$500, M + CO = \$300$, and reserve change is \$200. In the second situation, the change equals minus \$200.

The current account deficit ($CAD = M–X$) is being financed from two sources: Net capital inflow ($NCI = CI–CO$) and reserves of the central bank. In the case of flexible exchange, the exchange rate adjusts to eliminate any mismatch between demand and supply in the foreign exchange market. In the present context, the central bank is not allowing the exchange rate to change and the burden of adjustment falls on its foreign reserves.

The type of intervention in which RBI's purchase and sale of foreign exchange, causes changes in domestic monetary conditions, is called *unsterilized foreign exchange intervention*. Often, central banks do not want the domestic money supply to change as a result of their transactions in foreign exchange (exchange rate policy). This is because expansion in money supply, also known as a situation of easy liquidity, is dreaded for its possible inflationary effect. Central banks then have to undertake appropriate offsetting transactions in other assets. For example, the monetary impact of RBI's sale of $100 to X can be neutralized by conducting an open market purchase of government bonds worth Rs 4000. Neutralization of monetary expansion brought about by purchase of dollar, to prevent the exchange rate from falling, (rupee appreciation) will require open market sale of bonds or other assets. A foreign currency transaction coupled with an offsetting operation that leaves money supply unchanged is called *sterilized foreign exchange intervention.* Sterilization may be full or partial. Sterilization is full in our example because the change in money supply was completely neutralized. It would have been partial, if the sale of $100 (Rs 4000), was followed by purchase of bonds worth less than Rs 4000. In other words, sterilization is partial when the offsetting change is smaller in magnitude than the initial change in foreign reserves. Sterilization will not be necessary if the central bank did not care about the monetary implications of its exchange rate policy.

There are limits to the ability of the central bank to intervene in the foreign exchange market to support an exchange rate that does not clear the market. At such a rate, the BoP will be out of equilibrium. When the policy is to support an overvalued rupee (deficit in BoP), intervention may be halted as foreign reserves dwindle to zero. In the case of surplus in BoP, the limit may be unwillingness of the monetary authorities to continue adding to the stockpile of reserves or objections raised by trade partners against the country's artificially maintained surplus. China was in this situation in the middle of 2005. There was intense pressure by the US government on China to withdraw or relax its support of yuan. Without the support through massive purchase of dollars by the Bank of China, the yuan would have appreciated, thereby bringing down the country's trade surplus with the US. During 1986–7, the US pressured Taiwan, which was sitting on a huge pile of official foreign asset reserves, to go slow on further accumulation and allow its currency to appreciate substantially.

For the RBI, both the US dollar and the euro are intervention currencies. Foreign currency assets are maintained in major currencies like the US dollar,

Box 4   China's Mountain of Reserves

In 1994, China had switched from a system in which there were several exchange rates, each applicable for a particular type of international transaction, to a uniformly fixed rate of 8.28 yuan (also called the renminbi) per dollar. This stability induced by a fixed rate enabled it to weather the Asian crisis of 1997–8 with remarkable success. But as China's trade surplus (excess of exports over imports) with the US began to grow rapidly in the first part of 2000, it came under intense pressure from the USA to withdraw support, and let the yuan appreciate. A bill introduced in the Congress proposed to impose heavy duties on all imports from China, unless the yuan was allowed to become stronger. In July 2005, China changed the peg from 8.28 to 8.11 yuan per dollar with small variations around this target permitted. There is evidence that a larger revision was contemplated, but finally given up, to minimize the damage to Chinese exporters.

Since 2001, the Chinese government has had to participate in the foreign exchange market to buy dollars and sell yuan. This proved that the officially fixed rate was above the market-clearing level. If China had not done so, the pressure of high private supply of dollars (demand for yuan) would have led to a fall in the yuan–dollar exchange rate. Even at the new rate of 8.11, the yuan continues to be undervalued, because China's stock of foreign reserves keeps on increasing. Starting from $166 billion in 2001, the stock had climbed to $711 billion by mid-2005. Currently, it stands at a staggering $2435 billion. Most of it is invested in safe dollar assets like US government bonds. Therefore, a large part of China's trade surplus with the US is actually finding its way back to the US in the form of loans. When the credit rating of the US was lowered in 2011, it was a matter of deep concern for China.

China's policy change highlights a disturbing aspect of the international flow of funds. As pressure built on China to reduce the exchange rate, (raise the dollar per yuan rate) speculators wanted to change dollars into yuan at the old rate, so that they could make a profit by changing yuan back into dollars at the new exchange rate. A high proportion of the Bank of China's purchase of dollars has involved the buying of such speculative funds.

euro, pound sterling, Australian dollar, and Japanese yen. Conforming to international practice, the value of reserves is denominated and expressed in US dollars.

Liberalization has considerably stimulated the flow of investible funds into India. Capital outflow from the country has also gone up but has been outstripped by investments, particularly of the portfolio type, by foreign institutional investors like pension funds, mutual funds, insurance companies and hedge funds. This has tended to raise the demand for rupee relative to its supply in the currency market. Instead of letting the exchange rate appreciate (stronger rupee) in a free market, the RBI has chosen to fix the rate above its market–clearing level. Therefore it has to purchase dollars and add them to its stock of reserves. The resulting rise in money supply (liquidity) may cause inflationary forces to develop, producing a range of undesirable consequences. Over the past decade, RBI has consistently tried to sterilize surging capital inflows and drain liquidity from the system by selling government securities in the open market. Special assets, the so–called market stabilization bonds, were created for this purpose.

Sterilization through purchase and sale of government bonds is often supplemented by changes in other policy parameters that affect the money supply. The cash reserve ratio (CRR) set by the central bank is one such parameter. An increase in this ratio forces commercial banks to contract their credit creation or deposit expansion. A lowering in the ratio allows them to extend more credit on the basis of the same volume of reserves at the central bank. Therefore, the expansionary monetary impact of a BoP surplus may be offset by open market sale of bonds plus an increase in CRR. This practice is adopted when domestic markets for financial instruments, such as bonds and government securities, are thin or undeveloped. The RBI often uses the CRR as an instrument of sterilization.

Sterilization, however, entails some costs. We discuss two possible cases—sterilizing a deficit in the BoP and sterilizing a surplus in it.

In the case of deficit, the country is maintaining an exchange rate below its market-clearing level and the stock of foreign reserves is dwindling continuously. Therefore, this policy is sensible only over a short period. The cost of reserve exhaustion may be very high. Even before the reserves are completely exhausted there may be a speculative attack leading to a currency crisis. Speculative attacks will be discussed in more detail in Chapter 4.

In the event that the country is sterilizing a BoP surplus, suppose that India has landed in this position due to the policy of supporting an undervalued exchange rate. Here, the stock of foreign reserves will be rising. These reserves are typically invested in short-term US Treasury bills. These bills are very liquid (can be converted into dollars rapidly), but earn a very low rate of return. When the RBI resorts to sale of government security following its purchase of foreign exchange, it is effectively giving bonds to the public in exchange for dollars. The interest to be paid on these bonds is higher than the low yield earned on US Treasury bills. This differential entails a loss for the RBI, which is a fiscal loss to GoI, because the Bank's profits are transferred to the government. These costs can be quite substantial. Annual estimates of this cost in Latin American countries during the 1990s ranged from 0.25 per cent to almost 1 per cent of the national income. It is comparatively lower in India.

The ability to sterilize is limited by the central bank's stock of financial assets. As the RBI's stock of government securities began to dwindle along with mounting costs, an Internal Working Group on Instruments of Sterilization was formed to give advice on the introduction of new instruments of steriliza-tion. Market stabilization bonds were launched on the group's recommendation. Faced with similar policy dilemmas, the central banks of China, Malaysia, Poland, and South Korea have also experimented with new and less costly methods of sterilization.

To at least partially offset the costs associated with accumulating reserves, some Asian countries have started exploring alternative uses for their reserves. These are sovereign wealth funds (SWF) which are created when national governments invest part of their reserves to acquire global assets that yield higher long-term returns. For example, the China Investment Corporation (CIC) uses dollars to acquire energy assets such as oil, gas, and coal across the world. It has been suggested that India too should set up a SWF.

However, this may not be good policy. If instead of being held as cash or US Treasury bills, reserves are put into higher yielding assets, they do add to income, But risk also increases, because in case of emergency, it will take time to convert them into cash. They are less liquid than Treasury bills. Usually there is a trade-off between yield and liquidity of assets. In addition to CIC, China has diverted part of its huge reserves to inject funds into some of its state banks. South Korea has contemplated the possibility of investing reserves to improve its financial infrastructure. In contrast, despite burgeoning reserves, the RBI has so far been unwilling to divert funds to other uses or raise income at the cost of lower liquidity. Thus its portfolio remains heavily invested in liquid international assets which can be turned into cash at short notice. High risk aversion has stood it in good stead during periods of international financial turmoil and so the bank's policy is unlikely to change in the near future.

To drain the additional money generated by dollar purchase, the RBI also increases the CRR of commercial banks. Since the banks do not get any interest on their reserves at the RBI, this policy imposes a heavy cost on them. The lending rate may be pushed up to compensate, causing an adverse effect on consumption and investment spending. There may be an increase in the fragility of banks that are under financial stress. More generally, the policy is discriminatory in the sense that profitability of banks as a group suffers vis-à-vis non-bank financial intermediaries who do not have to satisfy any reserve requirements. Hence, CRR as an instrument of control, has been given up by most of the major developed countries.

Why Try to Influence the Exchange Rate at All?

Why try to manage the exchange rate at all instead of allowing it to be entirely determined in a free market for currencies? Under a flexible system, any disequilibrium in BoP will be automatically corrected through changes in the price of rupee and the domestic monetary situation will not be affected. Problems of constantly monitoring the exchange rate and carrying out appropriate sterilization exercises can be abolished at one stroke. Does the system of pegged exchange have any points in its favour? It does.

The whole idea of the managed float is that without any outside control, the market-determined exchange rate may fluctuate too much in response to changing market sentiments of private agents. Any boost in investors' confidence in home assets will cause a surge in inflow and cause the currency to appreciate. This may render exports non-competitive and force exporting activities to contract. The situation may be reversed if foreign investors suddenly decide to withdraw funds from home assets. The home currency will depreciate in consequence. Thus, volatility in the sentiments of investors will be directly transmitted to the exchange rate. This will introduce a large element of uncertainty in the production and investment plans of firms and consumption plans of households. This is the exchange rate risk of a trading country. The profits earned in pounds by an American company in the UK will suddenly shrink in dollar value if the pound depreciates relative to the dollar. Import plans will also be upset by unexpected changes in prices caused by unstable exchange rates. Exchange rate volatility adds to the uncertainty of producing for foreign markets or buying from foreign sources or investing in foreign assets and makes it difficult to plan into the future. Such unpleasant contingencies can be mitigated by the use of forward exchange contracts, but hedging does not eliminate risk completely and adds to the transactions cost of trading.

Second, when domestic banks and business enterprises have borrowed heavily in the international market, a sharp depreciation (causing a high jump in the domestic currency equivalent of their foreign currency liabilities) puts them in serious financial trouble. During the Asian Crisis of the late 1990s, this sort of adverse balance sheet effect led to widespread bankruptcies and the resulting financial crisis triggered a cumulative contraction process.

Third, depreciation pushes up the rupee price of imports and imports include many intermediate inputs used by industry and agriculture. Oil is the most prominent example. A depreciation adds fuel to the inflationary fire by raising the cost of such inputs. Exports do get a demand boost after depreciation, but the adverse cost push effect will be an offsetting factor to the extent that export activities also require imported inputs.

It is chiefly due to these reasons that most central banks allow the exchange rate to change in response to changing market conditions, but stand ready to intervene to prevent large swings in its value in either direction. International commerce and investment are best served by a stable medium of exchange that minimizes uncertainty and transaction costs. Fixed exchange rates, however, have one big drawback. They make a country vulnerable to speculative attacks that precipitate financial crisis.

India's intervention in the currency market has mostly been to prevent rupee appreciations than depreciations. The aim is to protect the competitiveness of the country's exports. This strategy is sensible, given that the Chinese authorities do not allow the yuan to appreciate.

Exchange Control and Convertibility

Foreign exchange operations by the central bank is not the only way of intervention in the currency market. The government may choose to apply more direct control on the use of foreign exchange. When everyone has free access to the market and there are no limits on the permissible volume of transactions, the country's currency is said to be fully convertible. Departure from it takes the form of some type of exchange control. In its most extreme form, all foreign currency receipts (for instance, dollars earned by exporting) must be handed over to the authorities. Anyone requiring foreign currency will have to apply for it. Less severe forms of exchange control limit access to particular types of transactions. Dollars may be unavailable, for instance, to finance import of luxury consumer goods. When use of foreign exchange is permitted for financing current import and export of goods and services only, the currency is said to be convertible on current account.

Capital controls of various types may place strict to mild restrictions on transactions related to international financial activities. In the presence of such controls, the currency ceases to be convertible on capital account.

Since the inception of reforms in 1991 in India, supporters of globalization have been urging the government to lift all controls and make the rupee fully convertible on both current and capital accounts. Current account convertibility was allowed in 1994, but capital controls are still in place. Two committees have looked into the issue and have prepared roadmaps for transition to convertibility. We return to this topic in the final chapter.

3

International Funds Flow and Economic Policy

We have seen that a central bank can influence the behaviour of the exchange rate through its operations in the currency market. In particular, it can prevent undesired currency appreciation in the wake of a surge in capital inflow by buying up an appropriate amount of dollars from the market. That is, it steps in as an additional source of dollar demand to supplement private demand and to mop up the extra supply that is flowing in from foreign investors.

But the effect of supporting the pegged rate at its old level can be obtained by stimulating private dollar demand too. This can be done in several ways. First, the government may make importing more attractive by lifting restrictions or reducing import duties.

Stimulus to import will boost dollar demand on the current or trade account. Import (M) is raised to absorb extra capital inflow (CI). Second, outflow of funds from the country may be encouraged by relaxing restrictions on the holding of foreign assets by domestic residents. Third, authorities can choose an easier monetary policy. Such a policy will reduce the domestic rate of interest. This has two effects. As loans become cheaper, consumer spending as well as investment spending by business will pick up. Some part of this higher spending will spill over into imports. At the same time, capital inflow tends to go down as the fall in the rate of return reduces the attraction of domestic bonds. The combined effect of rising M and falling CI will be to reduce the demand for rupees and ease, if not eliminate, the pressure on the exchange rate to fall.

The impact of monetary action on the exchange rate may be summarized as follows. An easy money policy (higher liquidity and lower interest rate) unambiguously raises the private demand for dollars as commodity imports as well as purchase of foreign assets rise. This creates pressure for the depreciation of the rupee. The opposite holds true for monetary tightening.

Monetary policy is not the only policy option available to a government. Fiscal action consists of changes in government spending and revenue, mainly tax revenue. An increase in government spending has a stimulating impact on an economy by raising the demand for goods and services produced by the private sector. A tax cut has a similar effect as it raises the disposable income of households and profits earned by business. Consumption and investment spending get boosted and national income increases. A part of this higher income will spill over into higher imports by households and business.

But with no change in the supply of money, expansionary fiscal action (higher public spending, lower taxes, or both) is likely to raise the domestic rate of interest. The return on domestic equity will also increase as all asset returns tend to move together. The interest rate rises because the government enters as a borrower in the domestic market for investible funds to finance its extra expenditure. This increase in the rate of return on home bonds (and equity) attracts capital inflow from abroad.

What is the impact on the currency market? The rise in imports raises the demand for dollars, while the

70

rise in capital inflow raises its supply. What is the net impact? That will crucially depend on the sensitivity of capital flows to changes in asset returns. This sensitivity is alternatively known as the *degree of capital mobility*. If sensitivity or mobility is high, the rise in the domestic interest rate will induce a large inflow of funds and this will outweigh the rise in dollar demand on the current account, and create pressure for rupee appreciation. In contrast, under low mobility, the higher inflow on the capital account is likely to be smaller than and outweighed by the increase in demand on the current account, and the pressure will be for rupee depreciation.

So it is clear that the degree of capital mobility has an important bearing on the outcome of domestic economic policy. We shall see that monetary action will lose effectiveness completely in one particular case.

Capital mobility is said to be perfect when domestic and foreign investors face no barriers in asset transactions. There are no taxes, subsidies, or other transactions costs and adjustment in portfolios can be done very quickly. This is an extreme assumption whose main usefulness is to provide a clear benchmark for analysis. Though extreme, it is not an altogether bad assumption because, driven by the forces of global-ization, capital markets all over the world are moving towards greater openness at a fairly rapid pace.

The chief implication of perfect mobility is that rates of return of similar assets will be equalized across nations through *arbitrage*. If the return is higher in country A than in country B, funds will be immediately withdrawn from B and invested in A. This will lower the return in A and raise it in B. The process of uninhibited arbitrage will end only when the two returns are brought to an equal level. This is just another application of the rule that price of the same commodity cannot differ between two locations if transport cost is negligible and there are no taxes or restrictions on the movement of goods. Traders will buy where it is cheap and sell where it is costly, thereby driving up prices where it is cheaper and lowering prices where it is more expensive. Thus the price gap will be eventually eliminated.

The ultimate returns on international assets depend not only on the rates of interest prevailing in the countries but also on the exchange rates between their currencies. Consider an Indian investor calculating the returns on a domestic bond and an American bond. The bonds have similar risk characteristics, so that relative attractiveness is determined solely by relative returns. A dollar appreciation will enhance the rupee value of the dollar yield on the American bond and this capital gain makes the American bond more attractive. The effective return on the foreign bond equals the interest rate on it plus the expected appreciation of the foreign currency, which is the same as the expected depreciation of the home currency. Thus, if the rate of interest in the US is 3 per cent and the dollar is expected to appreciate against the rupee by 2 per cent, the effective yield on the American bond is 5 per cent. The return on the Indian bond is to be judged against this composite return on the foreign bond. Under perfect capital mobility, arbitrage will ensure that the two returns will remain equal. Any divergence will be quickly eliminated by prompt repositioning of funds.

There are two important implications. First, investors will move out of the home asset if the home interest rate falls or the home currency is expected to depreciate. Thus, changes in expectations about the value of a currency may trigger inflow or outflow of funds even if interest rates (or stock prices) are not changing. Second, rates of return on comparable assets may not be equalized across countries even under completely free movement of capital. An interest rate of 6 per cent on the Indian bond can coexist with an interest rate of 4 per cent on the American bond without inducing arbitrage if the rupee is expected to depreciate by 2 per cent. Given the expected depreciation of the rupee, a higher interest return is required as compensation to induce investors to continue to hold Indian assets.

Monetary Policy, Funds Mobility, and Fixed Exchange

Unrestricted asset transactions deprive a country's government of the ability to simultaneously target its exchange rate and to use monetary policy to attain other economic objectives. Suppose that India has committed itself to a fixed rupee–dollar exchange rate. This eliminates any possibility of changes in the relative returns of Indian and US bonds caused by changes in the exchange rate. Perfect mobility then implies that Indian interest rates must closely match those in the US, otherwise arbitrage will be immediately triggered. If interest rates differ, investors will massively withdraw their funds from the country with the lower rate and put it in the country with the higher rate, confident that their gains would not be erased by any change in the exchange rate. But the rate of interest in the US, established by its central bank, is beyond the control of Indian authorities. Therefore, equality of interest rates implies that India cannot change its own interest rate as part of its own monetary policy. Since India and not the US is fixing the exchange rate, the RBI's monetary role shrinks to a single, passive action. Its task is to offset any incipient pressures on the rupee's exchange value against the dollar.

To understand this important point suppose that India is under a fixed exchange rate and has removed all restrictions on the international mobility of funds. Let the interest rate in the US be 4 per cent. Arbitrage will force the Indian rate to be 4 per cent as well. Suppose the RBI wants to implement an easy money policy to stimulate consumption and investment in the economy. For this, it purchases securities in the open market and increases the money supply in exchange. Let us assume that the domestic interest rate falls to 3 per cent as a result of monetary expansion. But this will trigger arbitrage in which investors will sell rupees and demand dollars to buy more American bonds which are now giving higher returns. There will be upward pressure on the exchange rate. Commitment to a fixed exchange rate will force the RBI to sell dollars and buy rupees to neutralize the pressure. This results in the withdrawal of the extra rupees that were initially put in as part of the easy money policy. Money supply begins to contract back to its original level causing the interest rate to rise in the process. Arbitrage will stop only when the domestic rate has returned to 4 per cent, the rate prevailing in the American market. The only effect of the initial open market operation of bond purchase by the RBI is to change the composition of its balance sheet. It is now holding more domestic bonds and less foreign reserves. Money supply and interest rate remain unaffected.

India could regain its ability to use monetary policy as an instrument in two ways, restricting capital mobility or making the exchange rate flexible. If cross-border asset trade can be restricted, arbitrage cannot bring about full equalization of returns and India's interest rate can be decoupled from the prevailing rate in the US. Restricted or imperfect mobility may be due to administrative or legal controls on financial transactions, making it illegal or very costly for residents to invest outside the country. Easy money policy in India will lower the interest rate, but investors will have limited ability to move funds from rupee to dollar in response to the difference in returns.

As domestic bonds become less attractive, some domestic investors move into foreign bonds by selling rupees. The RBI must step in to support the exchange rate but the foreign exchange intervention may be small compared to the initial open market purchase. Also if capital controls completely block any movement into foreign bonds, there may be no need for such intervention. Pressures in the currency market, under strong capital controls, are mostly limited to demand and supply driven by current account trade (X and M in equation 1) alone. Since the volume of current account transactions is much lower compared to capital account, these pressures can be normally handled without difficulty by buying or selling from the RBI's stock of dollars as necessary.

Thus with restricted fund mobility, a country has some freedom to set the domestic interest rate while maintaining the exchange rate. This freedom depends primarily on two factors. First, the degree of capital controls the country is able to impose on cross-border investments and, second, the amount of foreign reserves it holds. The larger the stock of reserves, the more it can afford the drain it is likely to suffer if it decreases the interest rate at a given exchange rate.

If capital controls are ruled out, the power of monetary policy may be restored by allowing the rupee–dollar exchange rate to be flexible. In that case, the RBI is free to lower the Indian interest rate, but the rupee will depreciate against the dollar as a result. If the interest rate is raised to dampen demand as an anti-inflationary policy, the home currency will appreciate and the export sector may be hurt.

The limitations that free capital mobility imposes on the exchange rate and monetary policy are often summed up as the *inconsistent or impossible trinity*. This is represented in Figure 6.

It is impossible for a country to simultaneously have unrestricted funds mobility, a fixed exchange rate and independent monetary policy. It must choose one side of the triangle, giving up the opposite corner. In reality, no country, India included, wants or tries to keep the exchange rate irrevocably fixed. The prevailing system is best described as a controlled float. But the point remains that under open capital movements,

78

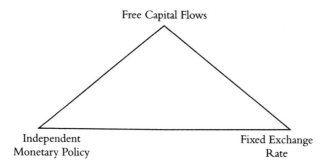

Free Capital Flows

Independent
Monetary Policy

Fixed Exchange
Rate

FIGURE 6   Impossible Trinity

greater the attention given to the exchange rate, the more constrained monetary policy is in pursuing other objectives.

In the wake of unexpected but short-lived disturbances, surplus or deficit may temporarily appear in the BoP. Political unrest in Egypt may disrupt India's exports to that country, causing a fall in the demand for the rupee from Egyptian importers. This will put upward pressure on the exchange rate but can be neutralized by policy intervention. Once Egypt returns to normalcy intervention may stop. Similarly, rice exports may show a seasonal pattern, increasing immediately after the harvest. The effect on the exchange rate is predictable and so is the required intervention.

Box 5   Capital Controls

Capital controls are restrictions on the ability of investors to move their funds in and out of a country. They are broadly of two types, administrative and market-based. Administrative controls either prohibit certain types of transactions outright or set quantitative limits. Market-based controls, on the other hand, discourage asset transactions by raising their costs. Two types of market-based controls are commonly used by emerging market economies—unremunerated reserve requirements (URR) and taxes. Under the former, investors are required to keep a fraction of their planned transactions in the form of deposits that carry no interest. In 1991, Chile decreed that 20 per cent of all incoming portfolio capital had to be put into a non-interest bearing deposit at the central bank up to a period of one year. This constituted a heavy penalty on inflows of short maturity. Subsequently, URR was successfully used by Colombia, Brazil, and Thailand during 2006–9.

So far India has mainly relied on administrative controls for both debt and equity inflows. Debt inflows are subject to ceilings. In the case of equity purchase, there is no overall limit, but a cap in terms of its proportion to a company's share capital is imposed. Prior to January 2012, only FIIs and non-resident Indians could directly invest in the Indian stock market. Now 'qualified foreign investors' or QFIs can also do so. QFIs are individuals or groups that meet certain pre-specified standards.

A major issue for supporting a fixed exchange rate is the length of time for which intervention must continue. Returning to Figures 1 and 2, temporary disturbances cause temporary shifts in the demand–supply curves. The curves return to their original position after the shock passes. Imbalance emerges but does not persist for long. Defending a target exchange rate can work well in such a situation. In case of surplus, the central bank steps in as buyer of foreign exchange and in case of deficit, sells from of its stock of reserves. If the stock is inadequate, dollars may be borrowed to meet the gap. Corresponding changes in the domestic money supply will also be temporary and may not have a noticeable impact on the price level. Without the danger of inflation, sterilization will also be unnecessary and the associated costs may be avoided.

The situation is radically different if the imbalance is fundamental and not temporary. Under a policy of defending a fixed rate, the central bank will continuously accumulate reserves if the imbalance is a surplus or continuously lose reserves if the imbalance is a deficit. In the latter event, the situation can be particularly dangerous.

Suppose that India is losing its competitive edge in its export market due to inflation which is pushing up domestic cost of production. As a result of declining exports, the demand for rupees or supply of dollars is falling steadily. In Figure 7, the supply curve of dollars is continuously moving to the left. In a flexible exchange situation, balance will be maintained by a continuous depreciation of the rupee. But the authorities do not want the exchange rate to change, possibly to avoid the harmful effect of depreciation on the balance sheet of domestic companies.

Prior to the onset of inflation, the exchange rate is OA, ensuring balance in the BoP. Let us focus on a particular point of time after the onset of inflation. Exports have fallen, pulling the dollar supply curve to a new position, which is to the left of the original. Without intervention, the exchange rate would be OB.

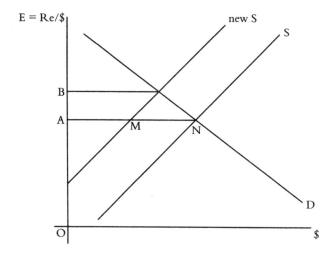

FIGURE 7   Effect of a Fall in Exports due to Inflation

However, the RBI wants the rate to remain at OA. At that level there is a deficit in BoP equal to MN. This gap must be met by selling dollars in the market. Since the situation persists, (which is why it is fundamental and not temporary) the depletion of official reserves will continue and eventually sink to a very low level. This may be treated as a very bad signal by international investors and the country's credit rating in the international market may fall. Foreign lenders may respond by reducing loans, demanding higher interest rates, or worse, a speculative attack on the rupee might begin.

An extremely low stock of foreign reserves undermines the ability of the country to defend its currency. This triggers the expectation of depreciation as soon as support is withdrawn, triggering in turn a rush to sell off rupees and buy dollars. One can make profits by selling those dollars when the price of dollar goes up after the imminent devaluation of rupee. For example, suppose that the current exchange rate is 40 but it is soon expected to increase to 45. If a speculator sells Rs 40 in exchange for one dollar now, she can sell it for Rs 45 after depreciation. Even if not interested in windfall profits, she may still want to move her funds out of Indian bonds into US bonds which have now become more attractive due to expected dollar appreciation. As people hasten to move out of the rupee, it becomes even harder for the RBI to defend the fixed rate. Its low stock of dollars will run out more rapidly and the expected devaluation becomes a certainty. The currency has succumbed to a speculative attack.

In the event of a speculative attack some countries try to defend their currencies by raising the domestic interest rates, often to astronomically high levels, in the hope that it will stop the flight away from the currency. But historically, in most cases, this type of attempted interest defense has failed to stem the tide of speculation. At the same time, by pushing up the cost of borrowing, it exerted a depressing effect on domestic production and employment. The RBI followed a tight money policy to keep interest rates high in response to the Asian crisis in 1997–8. This in addition to capital controls enabled India to tide over the crisis at relatively low cost.

The failed defense of the Mexican peso in 1994 clearly shows the high costs of intervention when BoP disequilibrium is not temporary. The domestic inflation rate was persistently higher compared to its main trade partner, the US. Current account deficit rose steadily, putting upward pressure on the peso. Political disturbance added to the pressure as investors sold off peso-assets and converted peso into dollar. But the authorities continued to stubbornly support the official rate of 3.5 pesos per dollar. The country's holding of reserves came down from over $30 billion to less than $6 billion in the course of a single year. With the dollar stock hitting rock bottom, the monetary authority was forced to surrender and the exchange rate jumped to

5 pesos per dollar by the beginning of 1995. There was severe recession accompanied by a large-scale flight of capital out of the country. Falling income improved the current account balance to some extent by reducing imports. Worried by the financial and political turmoil of its southern neighbour, the US, government stepped in with a rescue package that permitted the Mexican government to borrow up to $50 billion from the US and the IMF.

China's current position is the opposite of Mexico's in the early 1990s. Its overall BoP surplus has been persisting for decades and does not appear to be temporary. The US and European Union governments have been exerting great pressure for an appreciation of the yuan. In July 2005, a small revaluation occurred, but it was hardly enough to eliminate the surplus. The cost of rising reserves in terms of returns foregone continues to mount and so does the pressure from China's trade partners.

Tackling Fundamental Disequilibrium

If disequilibrium in BoP is not transitory in nature, the policy of intervention to support the exchange rate cannot be sustained for long. Take once again the worrisome case when the country is losing foreign reserves. The BoP is in deficit, implying that outflows M+CO exceed inflows X+CI at the pegged exchange rate. The foreign reserves will be eventually exhausted. To avoid such a situation, the country will have to take action to eliminate the deficit. This can be done most effectively on a permanent basis if an improvement in productivity and general efficiency can be realized. Improved productivity will bring down prices and this will have the effect of raising exports and lowering imports. Combined with low inflation, it will also entice a higher capital inflow and thereby enhance the supply of dollars. A low level of government debt is often taken as a sign of fiscal health of the economy by outside investors. Therefore, reining in such debt through reduction in budget deficit can be an effective instrument for stimulating inflows. A corruption-free environment and growing supply of skilled labour go a long way towards making the home country a more attractive destination for foreign capital. Thus, improvement in productivity and fiscal discipline, investment in skill formation, and control of inflation and corruption figure high among the set of policies that will enable a nation to keep its BoP problems firmly under control.

If the problem is one of chronic surplus, as is the case with China, an enduring solution will be to allow more imports of goods and services into the country. This will enhance the satisfaction of Chinese consumers by expanding their choice of consumption. Exports and capital inflows are ultimately a means to raising the standard of living of the citizens of a country. China's current thinking on trade policy seems to have put the cart before the horse by vastly overstating the positive role of exports as an engine of growth.

However, it is rather difficult to judge what constitutes fundamental disequilibrium in the balance of payments. How long and in what form should an imbalance persist before we can call it fundamental? There is unfortunately no clear answer that can be useful to policymakers as they chart their way in the turbulent waters of international finance.

We have seen that monetary policy becomes ineffective under full capital mobility and fixed exchange rate. What about fiscal or budgetary action? Is it still not available as a policy instrument? For instance, if the economy has run into recession is it not possible for the government to try to counter it by raising its own spending or by cutting taxes to stimulate consumption and investment spending? In principle yes, but in practice budgetary policies are difficult to change and put into action quickly in response to changes in domestic or international situations. Moreover, increase in fiscal deficit will make the government's debt larger. The burden of servicing the debt in future, paying interest, and repaying the principal will also be greater. Since no income-earning asset has been created against the additional debt, households and business may justifiably assume that taxes will be raised in future to meet the need of debt servicing. This may lead them to reduce current consumption and investment and neutralize, partially or even wholly, the impact of fiscal expansion.

The Role of the IMF

Central banks losing reserves in attempts to defend the exchange rate often turn to the IMF as a source of foreign currency. For instance in 1997, IMF loans to Thailand, Indonesia, and South Korea amounted to $17.2 billion, $58.2 billion, and $42.3 billion respectively. Next year it lent $41.5 billion to Brazil and $22 billion to Russia. If foreign investors believe that IMF loans are enough to stabilize the exchange rate, then speculative sale of the home currency and flight of capital out of the country may cease.

However, IMF loans carry some *conditionality*. Funds are released only if the country requesting the loan agrees to carry out important policy reforms which, in the opinion of the IMF, will improve economic performance and make repayment of the loan possible. Almost invariably, the IMF insists on fiscal reform—initiating cutbacks in public spending, removing subsidies, and raising taxes. The other important components of conditionality are monetary restraint, deregulation of domestic business, and privatization to unleash private initiative. Most loans are disbursed in installments over time and portions are withheld if performance criteria are not met. This kind of conditionality has generated heated controversy as the burden of expenditure cutbacks and subsidy elimination falls disproportionately on the poor and reduction in public spending tends to worsen the economic crisis. Owing to these undesirable consequences, governments are often reluctant to carry out the reforms demanded by the lender. Foreign investors correctly fear that non-implementation of reforms will lead to a scaling back of assistance and they continue pulling money out of the economy. The balance of payments position does not improve as a result. This was witnessed in South Korea in 1997. The government's promise to implement economic reforms lost credibility, capital outflow could not be arrested or reversed, and in spite of substantial lending IMF's intervention failed to work.

Critics have pointed out that the IMF is too inflexible in its policy stance and puts excessive focus on market-based solutions such as deregulation and privatization. Social welfare everywhere is a matter of efficiency and equity, but the IMF is concerned almost exclusively with efficiency, defined in very narrow terms. Global experience has made it abundantly clear that proper balancing of efficiency and equity under capitalism cannot be achieved without appropriate governmental supervision, but this has hardly been recognized by the IMF. No wonder, its attempts to reduce the role of the government have too often been responsible for exacerbating the social and economic instability of nations that were forced to approach it in times of distress.

4

Currency Crisis and the Convertibility Debate

The ability to borrow from international capital markets, in principle, should be an important source of gain for a developing country. Inadequate domestic resources can be supplemented by borrowing from abroad to stimulate investment, income, and growth. Resource inadequacy in a low-income generating country acts as a constraint not only on private borrowers, but on the government as well. Public expenditure on productive activities may not be undertaken because of lack of funds due to problems with tax collection and a host of other demands on the government's budget. This resource constraint on the public sector may be removed by selling government bonds to foreign investors.

In addition to initiating a positive cycle of investment and growth, capital mobility can improve social welfare by promoting policy discipline in developing countries. It is argued that the need to entice foreign investors and prevent capital flight will force the government to strive for stability in the economic environment and maintain international standards in policy implementation and corporate governance. For instance, nations that seek to attract capital are more likely to keep public debt, inflation, and corruption under control as investors place a high value on price stability and transparency.

In sharp contrast to this rather straightforward and rosy narrative, foreign borrowing in practice has often been a mixed blessing at best. Periods of sustained capital inflow have frequently ended in financial crisis. That the case for unfettered flow of private funds is not as straightforward as it seems, is clearly brought home by the perverse tendency of funds to move 'uphill', from the poorer to the richer nations.

Poor nations have much less capital than the rich ones and hence the returns to capital should be much higher in the poor countries. So one should expect a high flow of capital from the developed to the developing world. However, over the last three or four decades, the international movement of investible funds has been overwhelmingly between the industrialized countries. Still more perverse is that in recent years, substantial amounts of FDI have flowed from low-income to high-income countries. China, which is still a poor country, has been a leading capital exporter. Outward FDI from India, for example, Tata acquiring Corus in 2006 and Hindalco acquiring Novelis in 2007 is also on the rise. The apparent paradox vanishes once we recognize that scarcity of capital may not be the sole determinant of its returns.

The productivity of capital crucially depends on the availability of skilled labour, infrastructural facilities, and a country's law and order situation. Multinational enterprises are often tempted to set up production units in developing countries attracted by the availability of cheap labour. But their profit expectations may not be fulfilled if the supply of skilled workers is low and there are serious bottlenecks in transport, telecommunications, or power supply and the legal process of enforcing contracts, and punishing the guilty is painfully slow. There may be restrictions imposed by the government on the operation of foreign capital and the risk of a drastic change in policy following a change in the political situation may be quite high. Owing to these reasons, a developing country may not be an attractive destination for foreign investors despite its low capital stock. For the same set of reasons, even domestic investors, if given the chance, would like to hold foreign rather than domestic assets in their portfolios. This explains the apparently perverse flow of funds from the poor to the richer economies once restrictions on fund movements are lifted.

Indeed, instead of contributing to domestic stability through policy discipline, periods of sustained capital inflow have frequently ended in currency crisis. Such a crisis occurs when a country is forced to withdraw support from fixed exchange and there is sharp depreciation of the currency. This frequently leads to a banking crisis, evident during the Mexican crisis in 1994 and the Asian crisis three years later. The government's commitment, in each case, to a fixed exchange virtually eliminated the exchange risk of international transactions. The loosening up of capital controls enabled companies, banks, and government agencies to borrow overseas on a large scale. These funds were invested in infrastructure projects and other ventures that promised high returns in a growing economy. Matters seemed to proceed smoothly until political disturbances and irresponsible economic policy made investors lose confidence in the ability of the Mexican government to defend the peso. Throughout the 1990s, many Mexican individuals and companies as well as foreign investors began exchanging peso assets for dollar assets. The central bank spent more than $20 billion in 1994 from its dollar reserves to defend the home currency. Towards the end of the year, when the reserves were nearly exhausted, the bank stopped intervention in the currency market and the peso lost half its value.

It was expected that the large depreciation of peso would help Mexico by boosting exports, but this proved to be impossible owing to the negative effect on the balance sheet of banks and companies. As they had borrowed heavily in foreign currency, the liability side of their balance sheet suddenly doubled in terms of pesos. The result was widespread bankruptcy. Similar devastation occurred in Thailand and Malaysia following the sharp depreciation of their currencies. Many of the large customers of banks also had borrowed abroad and were hit hard by the jump in their debt servicing liabilities in terms of pesos. Some of these defaulted on their local loans as well, adding to the woes of the banks. Currency crisis thus quickly led to a more pervasive financial crisis. In turn the ruined banks stopped lending, investment and consumption spending collapsed, and the economy contracted sharply. Government spending was sharply cut back, interest rates rose sky high, and unemployment more than doubled. Disaster was averted only with the help of massive emergency loans orchestrated by the US government and the IMF.

Though this was the Mexican experience, most other crises essentially followed the same pattern. The Asian crisis can be said to have started with the devaluation of the Thai baht in July 1997. Here too change in expectations leading to a speculative attack and faulty government policy played a critical role. During the 1980s and the first half of the 1990s, the economies of Hong Kong, South Korea, Thailand, Indonesia, Malaysia, and Singapore grew at spectacularly high rates and attracted foreign funds on an ever increasing scale. Exchange risk was absent as the currencies were pegged to the dollar. Encouraged by this and enabled by the loosening of capital controls, total private capital inflows to Indonesia, Malaysia, South Korea, Thailand, and the Philippines jumped to $93 billion in 1996, up from $41 billion in 1994. However, a rapidly expanding portion of the inflow into Thailand was finding its way into speculation, particularly in real estate. Given implicit guarantees by corrupt government officials, banks and finance companies freely borrowed dollar and yen from foreign banks, and granted loans to speculators. Corruption was rampant due to weak government regulation and supervision.

A deep recession in Japan, accompanied by a falling yen, led to a sharp reduction in exports from this region. Under flexible exchange, this would have caused a fall in the value of the baht, but the authorities tried to defend the fixed rate by selling dollars. Soon it became clear that such intervention could not be sustained. Expectation of devaluation opened the floodgates to the sale of baht as short-term capital took flight. This rendered currency defense impossible. The eventual devaluation triggered a downward spiral owing to the adverse effect on the balance sheets on domestic companies and banks. Interest rates were pushed to very high levels to persuade investors to keep their money in the country, but these high interest rates themselves produced an economic slump. The IMF organized large rescue packages subject to conditionality. The packages plus the policy reforms did contain the crises, but not without significant costs.

The crisis in Thailand quickly spread to a number of neighbouring countries as foreign investors lost confidence and were joined by local borrowers in the scramble to sell the local currency. During the second half of 1997, the exchange values of the currencies of Thailand, Indonesia, South Korea and, the Philippines declined by as much as 40–50 per cent.

All the afflicted countries, except Malaysia, approached the IMF for assistance and received loans in return for implementation of economic reforms. However, despite IMF assistance, the recession continued well into 1998 and after. The IMF's role in managing the Asian crisis has come under serious criticism. Once a country was in the grip of crisis, IMF funds and programmes had not only failed to stabilize the situation, but in many cases made matters worse, especially for the poor. Thailand and South Korea were forced to further liberalize their capital markets, even though excessive short-term debt had been a principal cause of the trouble in the first place.

India weathered the storm rather well, chiefly because it has not opted for full liberalization of the capital account. Some countries that had liberalized to a greater extent considered the possibility of re-imposing restrictions. Malaysia did so and reaped immediate benefits in the form of a quicker and less painful recovery. Prior to the outbreak of the Asian crisis, the IMF was on the verge of modifying its Articles of Agreement to make the liberalization of private capital flows of all types its central target. As a result of the terrible turmoil this plan was put on hold.

Poor banking regulation was greatly responsible for the origin of the trouble in Thailand and its subsequent spread to Indonesia and the Philippines. Stricter supervision would have prevented banks and other financial institutions from the excessive risks they were undertaking using borrowed funds. Due to a lack of transparency in their operations, foreign investors and domestic depositors regarded the banks as safe solely because they believed that the government would stand behind them in trouble. Eager to ensure smooth funds flow to finance companies run by their relatives, government officials gave out signals to confirm them in their belief. This implicit guarantee from the highest level encouraged the banks to throw caution to the winds and take excessive risks in real estate ventures. In India, chiefly due to a very vigilant RBI operating in a relatively less corrupt environment, the standard of bank supervision has always been fairly high, and in fact much higher than in any typical developing country. This, coupled with controls over incoming short-term funds, succeeded in keeping speculation and destabilizing capital movements at bay. The RBI did follow a tight money policy, pushing up the domestic interest rate to keep capital at home. But this was more of a supplementary step and would have failed to be effective as an isolated measure. China could escape by keeping the doors shut on short-term private capital movements. Foreign investment has been usually restricted, almost exclusively, to FDI type flows which are long-term, stable, and not subject to sudden panics and reversals.

The turmoil in East Asia and elsewhere has made it clear that the developmental benefits of unfettered flow of funds are not automatic and may be easily undone by regulatory failure, corruption, and lack of reliable information. The crisis-prone downside of unrestricted movement of capital must be weighed against the potential gains in efficiency that would flow from such movement in a hypothetical crisis-free world. Sure enough, serious economic crisis can arise and has arisen even when capital markets are completely closed. However, it would be completely wrong to suggest that this somehow negates the fact that short-term borrowings and speculative flows under free mobility are likely to be, and have been, a source of major economic disturbance. Careful studies undertaken by economists have also failed to find conclusive evidence in support of the benefits of fully open capital accounts. There appears to be no clear pattern between the degree of capital account openness and the growth of an economy.

Nor is it true that free movement of funds is indispensable for prosperity and growth. Both Japan and China have succeeded in achieving high growth without unrestricted capital mobility. Barriers to capital transactions are still quite formidable in China. In Europe, except for Switzerland and Germany, most countries chose to retain extensive capital controls until the late 1980s. In the US, barriers to capital outflows were progressively raised over the 1960s.

The benefits of lending and borrowing might not be realized, even within a country, if the lenders hesitate to release funds due to lack of adequate information about the projects to be undertaken by prospective borrowers. The problem gets greatly magnified when the two parties are separated by international political borders, languages, and cultures. An American investor's costs of gathering relevant information and monitoring operations are much larger in West Bengal than in Iowa. To minimize the risk generated by inadequate or unreliable information banks, mutual funds and pension funds distribute their funds among a large number of projects in several countries. Although wide diversification does reduce risk, an undesirable consequence is that there is little incentive for fund managers to assess the quality of individual borrowers. Lack of proper knowledge also makes them susceptible to sudden panic and herd behaviour. This is exacerbated by the low cost of transferring funds from one country to another. Worse, since local borrowers know that foreign investors have imperfect knowledge about their activities, the temptation to cheat becomes very strong. The only deterrent that can possibly work is an alert regulatory body, which is often missing in developing economies.

Discriminating among Capital Flows

Since capital flows can be a potentially destabilizing force, it is important to differentiate between different types of flows with regard to their stability. Driven by considerations of long-term profitability, FDI is undertaken after careful cost–benefit analysis and, therefore, tends to be stable. It is difficult for investors to exit from enterprises in which they have acquired a controlling interest. Moreover, it is well-documented that FDI stimulates productivity and efficiency in the host country by acting as a vehicle for transfer of knowledge relating to technology and managerial practices. No such benefits flow from portfolio investment by institutional investors such as insurance companies, pension funds, and hedge funds. This is because such investment is primarily driven by expectations of capital gains generated by short-term movements in interest rates, exchange rates, or share prices. Since short-term expectations are swayed by ephemeral developments, undue panic or exuberance becomes the norm in currency markets. Portfolio inflows are supposed to stimulate investment by boosting share prices, but empirical evidence for India and other developing countries has failed to find any strong link between the stock market and domestic investment. There is strong evidence of foreign funds driving up prices in the real estate market, but this does not contribute to growth of productive capacity in the economy.

Short-term debt (maturity period of one year or less) may be a major problem if foreign lenders refuse to refinance it when it is due again. There is ample evidence that as soon as signs of trouble appear in the form of a dip in export prices or political uncertainties, bank loans are quickly liquidated and not renewed. Governments have tried to maintain foreign financing by raising the rate of interest, but this hurts local producers by raising the cost of borrowing and also raises the default rate on loans. Hence there is a clear need for strong government supervision that will prevent private borrowers from getting overexposed to short-term debt. Even the IMF now favours strict regulation of the flow of short-term funds.

The Convertibility Debate

One way the developing countries can insulate themselves against financial crises is to use instruments to control the movement of capital in and out of their economies. Such controls can take several forms, ranging from outright prohibition of private transactions in international assets (zero capital convertibility) to intermediate measures of varying control. Well-designed controls can help in achieving several major objectives. First, they can prevent the devastation associated with an economic crisis. They can ease the pressure on the local currency caused by capital flight by restricting the amount that can be taken out of an economy. Second, crisis in country A often causes investors to pull out funds from a healthy neighbouring country B in sheer panic, which plunges B in crisis through no fault of its own. Restrictions on capital outflow can significantly reduce exposure to such contagion. Third, controls can help in promoting desirable types of foreign investment. For instance, taxation of short-term capital will change the composition of inflows in favour of long-term, stable, and sustainable FDI-type investments. Finally, with capital controls in place, the difference between rates of return on domestic assets and foreign assets cannot be arbitraged away. This, in turn, returns power to the monetary authorities to set and alter the domestic rates of interest.

The controls on flows need not be quantitative, but may be in the form of tax on foreign loans. One form of such taxation, used very effectively by Chile in the 1990s, is to impose a requirement that some portion of short-term inflows be kept as interest-free deposit with the country's central bank for a specified period of time. The percentage of short-term inflows that was subjected to the mandatory requirement was not rigidly fixed, but changed by the government in response to changing circumstances. It started at 20 per cent in 1991, was raised to 30 per cent, then lowered to 10 per cent, and set to zero in 1998 when the flows nearly dried up.

Economists have intensely scrutinized the Chilean policy. As investors found ways of evasion by relabeling the flows as trade credit or loans supporting FDI, the authorities responded with stricter vigilance. Although the long-term impact on aggregate flows seems to have been insignificant, the tax was effective in lengthening the maturity of inflows. The share of short-term debt and portfolio investment, for which volatility is highest, declined steadily over time.

Notwithstanding the benefits of capital controls, they may not be first-best choice since other policy interventions that address the problems at source may be better. For instance, crises are often caused by excessive risks taken by local banks and other borrowers. In this case, the best policy response would be to strengthen bank regulation and supervision. But this cannot be achieved overnight and the use of capital controls can be justified as an interim measure. However, they tend to lose their effectiveness over time as pressures build up, and borrowers and lenders find ways to circumvent them. The best policy for a globalizing country would be to concentrate efforts on making its financial system robust and well-regulated before doing away with capital controls altogether, and making their currencies fully convertible.

Is India Ready for Full Rupee Convertibility?

There was intense pressure on the Indian government throughout the 1990s to liberalize capital transactions and make the rupee fully convertible on capital account. This is understandable because dollar interest rates prevailing abroad were much lower than domestic rupee rates, but Indian business was unable to take advantage of this source of cheap credit. The first Tarapore Committee (1997) proposed gradual liberalization spread over three years. It laid down three crucial preconditions for attaining full capital convertibility: fiscal consolidation, a mandated inflation target of 3–5 per cent per annum on an average, and strengthening of the financial system. The onset of the Asian crisis put the implementation of the recommendations on hold for several years. (The rupee was made fully convertible on *current* account in 1994.) It was evident that countries like India and China could escape relatively unhurt mainly because many capital restrictions were still in place. Malaysia's recovery could be expedited through the re-imposition of some critical controls. (Malaysia's Prime Minister Mahathir Mohammed described the global capital market as 'a jungle of ferocious beasts'!)

A new committee (Tarapore II) submitted recommendations for fuller capital convertibility, which was to be progressively achieved in three phases: Phase I (2006–7), Phase II (2007–9), and Phase III (2009–11). The major recommendations can be summarized as:

(a) Doubling of the limits on corporate investments abroad from the current level of 200 per cent of net worth

(b) Removal of ceiling of $22 billion on external commercial borrowings

(c) Allowing individuals to remit abroad annually up to $50,000 in Phase I, $100,000 in Phase II and $200,000 in phase III

(d) Allowing banks to borrow overseas up to 50 per cent of paid-up capital and reserves in Phase I, 75 per cent in Phase II and 100 per cent in Phase III

(e) Currently only NRIs are permitted to invest in companies listed in Indian stock exchanges. Extension of this facility is recommended to all non-residents through Securities and Exchange Board of India (SEBI) registered entities.

Also the two recent committees—The Expert Committee on Making Mumbai an International Financial Centre formed in 2007 under the chairman-ship of P. Mistry and the Committee on Financial Sector Reforms under the chairmanship of R. Rajan formed in 2008—have called for further deregula-tion of the capital account and of the financial sector. Some of these recommendations have already been implemented.

Is India ready for full convertibility? In our judgment, the potential risks may far outweigh the potential benefits. We have seen that unavailability or imperfection of information may lead foreign investors to lend too much money, even into unprofitable projects. Poorly supervised or inexperienced banks may end up allocating funds to wrong sectors and may be tempted to borrow more to cover losses. Ability to borrow from abroad may encourage reckless speculative lending by domestic banks. If this is abruptly halted by the refusal of foreign investors to give further loans, banks may become insolvent and a crisis may be triggered. India thus needs to strengthen its financial system by first erecting a proper supervisory framework. In recent years, a positive development in this area has been the decline in the percentage of non-performing bank advances. This ratio, possibly the best indicator of the health of the banking system, has significantly come down from its high value of around 14 per cent in 1997.

Unfortunately, the prospects are not so good with regard to public debt and inflation. High levels of public debt and inflation tend to make any growth process unsustainable and lower the confidence of foreign investors. The first Tarapore Committee rightly specified fiscal discipline and control of inflation as essential preconditions for full convertibility. Although fiscal discipline has improved considerably in the wake of the Fiscal Responsibility and Budgetary Management Act (FRBMA), the government's deficit is still beyond acceptable level and public debt as proportion of GDP continues to grow. And despite persistent targeting by the RBI, inflation rate remains high. Without substantial improvement in these areas, a quick move to complete deregulation would be premature. The second Tarapore Committee appears to have underestimated the magnitude of the costs of possible financial crises.

Fuller convertibility would be facilitated by greater flexibility in the exchange rate, as fluctuations in capital inflows and outflows would be cushioned by changes in the exchange rate and the need for RBI's intervention to buy or sell forex would be lower. The costs of maintaining high reserves would be lower as well. Thus, a move towards full liberalization should be accompanied by a relaxation of the policy of exchange rate management. The exchange rate should be left to be determined by the forces of demand and supply in the open market, unless surges in inflows and outflows are large and abrupt enough to cause large and unexpected fluctuations in it.

With a well-designed framework to regulate cross-border asset transactions, India can successfully achieve the following objectives: prevent the disastrous consequences of banking and currency crises, enhance national autonomy by reducing the influence of external factors on domestic decision-making, and promote desirable types of investments such as FDI which are stable, productive, and sustainable in the long run. If we can improve the quantity and quality of our physical and social infrastructure, the functioning of our legal system, and succeed in putting curbs on fiscal indiscipline and inflation, foreign investors will find India an attractive destination for their funds even under limited capital mobility. Indeed, both India and China, without full capital account liberalization, continue to be among the fastest growing economies in the world today.

Capital Flows and Exchange Rate Management in India during the Recent Global Crisis

In the wake of the US sub-prime crisis, India experienced a sharp reversal of the prevailing trend of

114

increasing inflows witnessed over the past decade. This adverse experience was shared by almost all emerging economies, as in a panic-driven response to heightened uncertainties, the investors rushed to pull out funds from their financial markets. It is interesting to note that despite the fact that the US was the epicentre of the crisis, given the depth of its financial market, it was still considered the safest haven by investors.

Net capital inflow into India fell by a staggering 69 per cent in the second quarter of 2008 and by almost 79 per cent in the third quarter compared to their values in the two quarters of the previous year. In the fourth quarter, the worst phase of the turmoil, net inflows actually turned negative (at minus $6 billion). This period was also characterized by an uninterrupted decline in share prices, with the BSE SENSEX nosediving from 19,829 in the fourth quarter of 2007 to 9,341 in the first quarter of 2009. It was only in the second half of 2009 that foreign funds started flowing back to India and the stock market also recovered.

The RBI was forced to sell forex in the final quarter of 2008 to cushion the impact of the huge capital outflow on the exchange rate. In addition to the possible adverse effect of negative balance sheets, it was

115

feared that the strong depreciation of the rupee would generate significant inflationary pressures by pushing up the cost of oil and other imported inputs. So RBI chose to sell almost $18 billion from its reserves; but despite the heavy sale, the rupee depreciated by almost 25 per cent. So great was the pressure unleashed by the flight from the rupee. Foreign exchange sale continued during the first and second quarters of 2009, but the amounts were far lower. Addition to reserves resumed in the second half of 2009 to counter the effect of enhanced inflow of funds.

However, the recovery of inflow was confined only to net portfolio investment, which jumped from minus $15 billion dollars (amounting to an outflow of $15 billion) in 2008 to $20 billion in 2009. The experience of the other categories between the two years was as follows: FDI from $23 billion to $18 billion, external commercial borrowing from $12 billion to $3 billion and suppliers' credit (short-term loans) from $6 billion to $0.1 billion. Of these, the drying up of suppliers' credit and the steep drop in external borrowing had the most serious impact on domestic production and investment. Without the sharp fall in the value of the rupee, the contractionary impact of the drop in export

116

demand and drying up of some types of short-term loans would have been much stronger.

The global crisis between September 2008 and late 2009 was the severest one since the Great Depression of 1929. But the Indian economy showed remarkable resilience and started to pick up growth momentum from early 2009, while the rest of the world was still steeped in stagnation. Did the recovery of FIIs play any role in this remarkable turnaround? Did the Indian corporate sector, taking advantage of rising share prices, generate investment by issuing new shares?

In the absence of any convincing evidence to suggest an affirmative answer, the role of FII recovery as the driver of the general recovery seems to be inconsequential. In India's case at least, higher portfolio inflow appears to be a liability on balance since it harms exports by causing an appreciation of the rupee. The most important factor contributing towards resilience of the economy was the strength and robustness of the domestic financial system. Compared to their counterparts in the advanced countries and other emerging economies, Indian banks had healthy balance sheets with near zero exposure to the 'toxic assets' originating in and propagated by the US financial sector. Capital

117

controls of various types were in force including limits on external borrowing by the corporate sector. In addition, the predominance of government-owned entities in the financial sector went a long way in preventing erosion of depositors' confidence and the emergence of systemic troubles that engulfed the US and the EU so quickly. The virtues of a relatively well-functioning and well-regulated financial system were highlighted as never before.

There are clear signs that these virtues have gained global recognition in the wake of the crisis. In fact, it is a regaining of the recognition they had once widely enjoyed. In the decades following World War II, financial regulation and restrictions on the movement of cross-border funds were universally accepted as essential tools of economic management. This was followed by a complete attitude reversal and the developing world was urged to do away with these 'barriers to efficiency'. Just before the outbreak of the Asian crisis, the IMF was poised to make the liberalization of all international private capital flows its central purpose and to extend its jurisdiction to capital movements. This sweeping programme was halted by that crisis.

Even then, when Malaysia imposed stringent controls to contain the forces of disruption, the IMF called this 'a step back' and an article in the international business press stated that 'foreign investors in Malaysia have been expropriated and the Malaysians will bear the cost of their distrust for years'. However, enough evidence accumulated to show that compared to other countries in the region, Malaysia's loss was lower and recovery, faster. This led the IMF to soften its stand on capital controls in subsequent years.

The latest crisis has brought controls back into the programme of economic management with a vengeance. The agreement signed by Iceland, that marked the biggest financial rescue in Western Europe in the past half-century, included provisions for strict capital controls. Latvia also was allowed to maintain the pre-existing restrictions. A joint World Bank–IMF report (2009) on the global meltdown noted that six countries namely, China, Colombia, Ecuador, Indonesia, the Russian Federation, and Ukraine imposed various types of restrictions on inflows and outflows during the crisis. Argentina, Venezuela, and South Korea also introduced controls on outflows as precautionary measures. Interestingly, the response of investors, the business press, and credit rating agencies was one of silence or tacit approval. The dramatic revival of the protective role of capital controls is likely to be among the lasting, positive legacies of the current global turmoil.

Conclusion

By developing country standards, the management of capital flows and the exchange rate by India has been exceptionally good. The RBI has successfully prevented excessive volatility in the value of the rupee vis-à-vis the major currencies and 'orderly conditions in the forex market' have been largely maintained. Thanks to its overall supervision, we have managed to avoid financial crises with their devastating attendant costs. The country's international credit rating is fairly good at present.

Commendable as this success is, it should not lead to complacency and lowering of guards. Eternal vigilance is the price of stability in the turbulent environment of international finance. Several points of serious weakness remain. Capital inflow is dominated by portfolio

investment in the stock of a small number of top per-
formers in search of quick capital gain. Surges in inflow
and upward movement of share prices have displayed a
positive correlation, but there is little evidence of any
link between the stock market and real investment in
productive capital. The composition of inflows needs
to be changed in favour of FDI. Vast amount of dollar
reserves invested in US Treasury bills and yielding a
very low return, have to be maintained for purposes of
'prudence and stability' because it is FPI and not FDI,
that still makes up the bulk of the inflow. Given the
sorry state of power generation and distribution and the
low quality of roads, ports, and other urban infrastructure, FDI has tended to be concentrated in information
technology (IT) and information technology-enabled
services (ITES) to take advantage of progress in telecommunications. The impact on general social welfare
would have been higher if the investment had taken
place in traditional manufacturing that uses labour
more intensively and has better links with the rest of
the economy.

The first Tarapore Committee laid stress on three
conditions for achieving economic strength and
stability—fiscal consolidation, control over inflation,

and a robust banking system. Of these, financial reform is in progress but far from being complete, and the other two are still off the mark. Therefore, irrespective of the high stock of foreign reserves, the regulatory mechanism for capital flows should not be hastily dismantled. In the wake of the recent global meltdown, such dismantling is unlikely to happen.

The Indian foreign exchange market is still quite shallow, characterized by uneven flows, and a few big players. As the market develops, participants are better able to manage their own micro risks and the RBI can concentrate on managing the economy-wide macro risks. Herd behaviour is far more likely in underdeveloped markets. Numerous measures have been initiated to enhance the efficiency of the currency and capital markets.

Foreign investment, mostly of the short-term portfolio variety, has not yet produced any positive impact on efficiency and growth in our economy. Share prices have tended to move in line with these flows, but there is no evidence of any link between the stock market and domestic capital formation. It is now easier for companies to use external borrowing for investment purposes, but there is a need for scrutiny and control to prevent short-term external debt from increasing too much in relation to national income.

According to the RBI: 'The basic objective has been to maintain orderly conditions in the financial markets and to ensure that capital flows promote efficiency without having an adverse impact on economic stability.' The first half of the objective has been achieved with a fair measure of success, but not the second.

References

Bhagwati, J. (1998), 'The Capital Myth: The Difference between Trade in Widgets and Dollars', *Foreign Affairs*, May/June, 77 (3): 7–12.

Fieleke, N. (1994), 'The International Monetary Fund 50 Years after Bretton Woods', *New England Economic Review*, September: 17–30.

Kindleberger, C. and R. Aliber (2005), *Manias, Panics and Crashes: A History of Financial Crises*, Fifth edition. New Jersey: John Wiley & Sons.

Nachane, D. (2007), 'Liberalization of the Capital Account: Perils and Possible Safeguards', *Economic and Political Weekly*, 8 September, 42 (36): 3633–43.

Pugel, T. (2008), *International Economics*, Thirteenth edition. Tata McGraw Hill.

Rajan, R.S., Sasidaran Gopalan, and Rabin Hattari (2011), *Crisis, Capital Flows and FDI in Emerging Asia*. New Delhi: Oxford University Press.

Rakshit, M. (2002), *The East Asian Currency Crisis*. New Delhi: Oxford University Press.

———. (2009), *Money and Finance in the Indian Economy*. New Delhi: Oxford University Press.

Sikdar, S. (2006), *Contemporary Issues in Globalization*, 2nd edition. New Delhi: Oxford University Press.

———. (2011), *Principles of Macroeconomics*. 2nd edition. New Delhi: Oxford University Press.

Stiglitz, J. (2002), *Globalization and Its Discontents*. USA: W.W. Norton and Company.

Van den Berg, H. (2010), *International Finance and Open Economy Macroeconomics*. New Jersey and London: World Scientific Publishing Co.

Further Reading

Chapter 1

Data on global capital flows and exchange rates can be found in Global Development Finance and *World Development Reports* published by the World Bank and *International Financial Statistics* published by the IMF. For India, annual *Economic Survey*s of Government of India and RBI's *Handbook of Statistics* on the Indian economy are the most frequently used sources of data and information. For a general discussion of the different facets of globalization from an economic perspective, Sikdar (2006) may be consulted.

Chapter 2

An accessible introduction to the material of this chapter is provided by Sikdar (2011). Rakshit (2009) contains comprehensive essays on management of foreign exchange reserves and policies relating to foreign institutional investment in the Indian context. Rajan et al. (2011) is a good read on private capital flows in emerging Asia.

Chapter 3

Sikdar (2011) and Pugel (2008) discuss the material covered here in more detail. Fieleke (1994) discusses the objectives and activities of the IMF. Stiglitz (2002) sets out a strong critique of the IMF.

Chapter 4

Kindleberger and Aliber (2005) present a very readable overview of financial crises over the centuries. A comprehensive discussion of the Asian crisis is found in Rakshit (2002). Bhagwati (1998) forcefully argues that the claims of enormous benefits from free funds mobility across national borders are not persuasive. The deep financial crisis of 2008–9 and the need for reform of the international monetary system are discussed in Van den Berg (2010). For a good treatment of different aspects of capital account liberalization in India, see Nachane (2007).

Index